Sheila

A
Company
of
Women

A
Company
of
Women

JOURNEYS

THROUGH THE

FEMININE

EXPERIENCE

OF FAITH

EDITED BY IRENE MAHONEY, OSU

TRIUMPH™ BOOKS
Liguori, Missouri

Published by Triumph™ Books
Liguori, Missouri
An Imprint of Liguori Publications

Library of Congress Cataloging-in-Publication Data

A company of women : journeys through the feminine experience of faith
/ edited by Irene Mahoney.
     p. cm.
     ISBN 0-89243-923-8 (pbk.)
     1. Ursulines—United States—Biography. 2. Spiritual biogra-
phy—United States. 3. Ursulines—United States—Spiritual life. 4. Women
—United States—Religious life. I. Mahoney, Irene.
BX4543.7C65   1996
271'.974022—dc20
[B]   96-18407

FOR OUR FOREMOTHERS

*...by day a pillar of cloud to guide them
on their journey; by night a pillar
of fire to give them light.*

—Exodus 13:21

Contents

Prologue

Act, move, believe, strive, hope, cry out to him with all your hearts,
for without doubt you will see marvelous things.

—SAINT ANGELA, PROLOGUE TO THE COUNSELS

In the summer of 1994 eight American Ursulines gathered together in the Ursuline Center in Cleveland, Ohio, for a purpose at once clear and mysterious: to tell journey stories. We had been surfeited by statistics about religious women, by sociological implications of our dwindling numbers, by psychological insights into our motivations, by theological reflections on our spirituality. All well and good, we said; but what about the persons behind the statistics? What about the individual experiences of our spiritual journeys?

We knew from the beginning that despite our common religious heritage our stories would be widely (and wildly) diverse, but it was not until we had lived and shared with one another through a long hot summer that we realized not only the uniqueness of the initial call, but the uniqueness of the path followed in each commitment.

We came from six different Ursuline congregations and from various geographical locations: Canada, Mexico, Belgium, Kentucky, Ohio, New York, Montana. We were lawyers, teachers, administrators, archivists, missionaries. We ranged in age from forty to seventy. Most of us had never met. Were we hoping for too much in expecting that we could plumb our experience, share our stories, and then take the perilous leap of writing them—all in a single summer?

That first Sunday we gathered after dinner in the large air-conditioned room which the Cleveland Ursulines had generously appointed for our use. We were awkward and shy with one another. Divested of our usual roles, we glanced around furtively looking for some way to cover our insecurities. In a classroom or a board room or even a court of law we would have known how to position ourselves. But here, now, with the dauntingly unfamiliar goal not only of becoming writers but of writing about ourselves—about what was most dear, most revealing, and most secret—no wonder panic vied with hope.

The room itself (a room that came to nurture us like a womb) seemed to our anxious eyes hostile and barren: large tables, large chairs, computer outlets, air conditioners. In that ascetic atmosphere there was little to distract us and, in those first hours, we longed passionately for distraction.

Working together in this austere environment was to be our first challenge. It was clear that we did not want to be together, that we wanted private space. Writers, above all others, needed a "room of one's own"—a place where our thoughts, our memories, our emotions, could be protected. Our stories were too fragile for a public space.

Little by little, however, we came together, silently at first, finding comfort in the common click of our computers, our common sighs, our common periods of "blank." Our room, once viewed as sterile and forbidding, became our sacred space, a silent setting that freed us to create.

An antidote to those long silent hours was our meals together. To our surprise we found ourselves to be natural storytellers, sharing our lighter memories with spontaneous delight. Laughter was at once a release and a bonding. So raucous were we one day that we suddenly realized all twelve tables in the dining room were turning to stare at us—not in disapproval, but simply curious at so much laughter. Such storytelling was a natural avenue to deeper sharing.

Our first days when panic vied with hope gave way to a steadier atmosphere. Day by day our summer became a graced and sacred time for us. Our task often demanded more than we thought possible to give. It demanded days of solitary reflection during which we spread out our geography and retraced the mountains and the deserts. Facets of our journey we had never truly claimed were acknowledged and given their rightful place. We gathered up the years, finding lovely patterns where in the living we had seen only chaos. Of course, there were also memories of bewildering pain, anger, bereavement. Sometimes in tears we relived moments when the only "sensible" decision would have been to throw off our veils, close the door behind us, and seek a less supernal vocation.

Such reflection was but the first step. The next was to share that story with our companions. Slowly our initial fear and distrust diminished as we experienced the gentleness and thanksgiving with which our stories were received. Our sharing sessions, taking place in the quiet of late afternoon, became the most precious time of the day, the period that strengthened and encouraged us for the demanding task of writing.

By the end of the summer we had completed our essays. One of our members entitled hers "One Ordinary Life." In one way it is a title appropriate to all our stories. None of our journeys are flamboyant unless, in a world where fidelity is so rare, commitment itself is flamboyant. Over and over we asked ourselves what had kept us steady. Grace, of course—whatever that elusive word means—and a bedrock faith that the commitment we had once made was worthy to be honored. And then the last ineluctable fact: that God who always honors his commitments had been faithful to us.

So we offer these as journey stories, narratives of ordinary lives, lives of commitment to a religious ideal—an ideal reinterpreted, reassessed, restructured, but with one unchanging reality: "We know in whom we have believed and we are certain that he is able to safeguard until that Day what we have entrusted to him" (2 Timothy 1:12).

Irene Mahoney, OSU

Turning Toward the Light

IRENE MAHONEY, OSU

*I know the plans I have for you, says the Lord, plans for welfare
and not for evil, to give you a future and a hope. Then you will
call upon me and come and pray to me, and I will hear you. You
will seek me and you will find me.*

—JEREMIAH 29:11-13

I have often wondered what it would be like to take stock
of my life, not in little snippets, but in its entirety. What would
the past look like—not as it existed in the past, but as it exists
now in my present? I am wise enough to know that I can
never recapture that past. Nothing was exactly the way we
remember it. More frequently than not, remembrance is a
lie. I know that I can never recapture the past. Nothing ever
was, in fact, the way we remember it. Remembrance, more
frequently than not, is a lie. And yet it is the only truth we
have on which to build our present—and our future—for it is
through the weavings and interweavings of past events that
we are led to fresh interpretation and vision.

The person who entered the Ursuline Order in October of
1942 is long gone. Even the chemicals which shaped that
body have, so the scientists tell us, been replaced. I remember
that girl, but less as myself than as a character in a rather
engaging novel. She was tall and dark, with gray heavy-lidded
eyes that in her adolescence she cherished because they seemed

to her "mysterious." She was attractive, though far from beautiful. She had an air of detachment, a coolness; she was, to use a French word that she loved, *dégagé*. The air, of course, was deceptive. She was far from the poise and sophistication she worked so resolutely to portray. It was not nonchalance, but the reticence of fear, of being caught, found out. That fear—the fear of being known for what she was—was as close as her skin. As far as she could remember, she had never been without it. Perhaps she hoped that religious life would free her from this constraining burden. Only as she grew older (and wiser) did she accept the ultimate fact that only God's creative presence could deliver her from her fears.

According to the few remaining photographs, she was a solid little girl with straight dark hair, even teeth, and a look of determination. Her father looked like a prosperous business man, with his navy suit and short clipped mustache. Her mother was dark and thin, with direct gray eyes and a rigid posture. The unusual thing about the little group was the age of the parents: the father was close to sixty; the mother was forty-seven. He had seven children from an earlier marriage; this was her first child—and she was fierce as a tiger to protect her. The Child had clearly been a surprise—not an unwelcome one, but a surprise, nevertheless. Perhaps in some mysterious way the Child had felt this and had already sensed herself to be an alien on coming into a world that had not expected her.

Her first five years were spent in Brooklyn, New York, in a large brownstone house. Just before her sixth birthday her parents moved to Long Island. Her father had retired from his job in the New York City Police Department and had accepted the responsibility of setting up a small police department in a recently incorporated village. Of that move she remembers nothing except the bewilderment of packing and her mother's angry grief that a beautiful mirror had been broken by the careless movers. The house to which they moved was a poor substitute for what they had left. It was small, badly equipped, and on an unpaved road.

To her mother it would never become home. To her father none of this mattered. He reveled in living "in the country." Across from them was a large meadow with a wide creek running through it. It was a haven for rabbits and birds of every variety. Her father never tired of walking through it or sitting on their porch gazing across at it and listening to bird sounds. Her mother, although brought up in a small town in northern New York, did not share his enthusiasm. The country was not her metier and the small, awkward house was a constant source of frustration and humiliation. For her everything made domestic life more difficult. There were no nearby stores or public transportation and since she did not drive, she found few escapes except for occasional trips to New York City to visit her sisters who had belittled her marriage from the beginning.

As for the Child, her first vivid memory was of standing in their driveway with her father. It was evening and it was cold enough for her to have on a sweater. From the meadow across the road rose a flock of birds. They were black against the sky and came straight for the Child and her father. The noise was terrible and she screamed in terror, hiding her face in her father's arms. He laughed and nuzzled her, whispering, "They're only crows; they won't hurt you." But giving them a name was not enough to allay her terror. It was her first remembered experience of those moments of terror which would continue to grip her beyond reason.

The community into which they moved was another source, if not of fear at least of alienation. It was a community of the rich, and even at the age of six, the Child knew that she did not belong. She was simply the child of a civil servant whose status was not very different from the grooms and gardeners employed on the estates.

The community, ideally situated, was enclosed between two bodies of water—Long Island Sound on one side and on the other a small, tranquil inlet with the unlikely name of Conscience Bay. The land jutted out into a point and there on a rocky cliff stood a manned lighthouse. As the Child grew older, this became her favorite place. She loved the excitement of walking there with her father, standing against him on the edge of the cliff, looking down at the water slipping over the giant rocks as the tide came in. Sometimes, toward evening, they would walk across the grass to the lighthouse and the lighthouse keeper would lead her up the winding stairs to where the beacon was, encased in a huge glass bubble. Mr. Rae would light the long taper and then carefully pass it to her and she—she—would light the light that all during the night would flicker and flare and save the world from destruction.

Mr. Rae was small and wiry and lived alone. The story (she couldn't remember where she had heard it) was that he and his wife had once been assigned to a lighthouse twenty miles from shore, accessible only by boat, and during bad weather not accessible at all. Here, the story goes, his wife went mad during a violent and prolonged storm. When they were finally able to get her to shore, she had to be brought to an asylum. She was still there, they said, with no hope for recovery. The story made the Child shivery and, at night when the wind was loud, she would imagine the terror of the woman, crouched in her lonely exile, battered by the sea and the howling wind.

That fall she began first grade in the public school of a neighboring town. Since their community was completely residential, it had no school of its own. There was no bus service in those days, so her father brought her each morning and came for her each afternoon. All the children brought lunch and ate in their classrooms. Many of them came from the large potato and cauliflower fields in the area. They were, for the most part, Eastern Europeans with unpronounceable names and funny things for lunch. There were some other children too; their parents were "the natives," old settlers who prided themselves on having lived in these waterfront communities for years. Some of them dated back as far as the Revolutionary War and there was a strong, prideful chapter of the Daughters of the American Revolution. With her Irish name and an address that placed her outside the school district, the Child found herself doubly alien.

She soon became aware of another stigma: she was Catholic. Catholicism was anathema to the "natives," who were for the most part staunch and exclusive Methodists. As for the Polish and Lithuanian children, although they were Catholic, their language and their ritual made them seem doubly removed from her. The first humiliation for being a Catholic came at school with the awarding of monthly prizes. Any child who had been on time every day for the month was given a small print of some well-known classic. Although she never missed school, she was occasionally late because of a Catholic holy day and, therefore, was excluded from receiving the award. Her father assured her that it was an honor to be a Catholic and that she should be happy at this little sacrifice. But she saw no sense in it. What was the honor? To be excluded from winning prizes? to drive every Sunday to a smelly, cold, little building where a small rotund man with a thick Dutch accent did magic things that made them all bow their heads? If there was honor in this, she could not find it.

Despite her frustrations, she loved school. She loved reading and learning new words. She liked being praised and knowing the answer when no one else raised a hand. And she loved her teacher who spoke to her about things she could understand.

When June came and school was coming to an end, she was desperate. With childish ingenuity she arranged to make school last longer. She told her father that she had to come every day for special work and to help the teacher. She arrived promptly with her lunch box, explaining to her teacher that her parents were both out and that they wanted her to stay in school until they could pick her up in the afternoon. For three days the ruse worked. On the afternoon of the fourth day, her father discovered what she had been doing. They drove home in silence. Although later that evening she could hear her parents talking about what she had done, neither of them ever spoke to her about it. The habit of passing through crises in silence was to be a family characteristic.

Perhaps this is the place to mention family. There were, as I have said, seven other children in the family—offspring of her father and his first wife who had died when the youngest child was only seven. She was—as far as one can gather— (remember: this is a family of silences) a fun-loving Irish woman who enjoyed her children, enjoyed her neighbors, was merry even in the midst of sickness. Her children were like her: short, sandy-haired blue-eyed people, garrulous and spontaneous.

Although most of them were old enough to be on their own when the Child's parents married, even so, resentment at a stepmother was palpable. How could it be otherwise? In place of their lighthearted mother had stepped this tall dark woman; a woman used to authority—punctilious, reserved, cautious. Especially cautious with them, for to her they were like a foreign country. They resented her for any number of reasons but mostly because she had the upper hand, the ace: she had given their father a Girl-Child in his old age. And on this Child he doted without distraction. As for the Girl-Child herself, it was not hard for her to pick up the climate of wariness where she was concerned. If she had her father's blood, it did not show; she looked every inch her mother. Only much later did she realize how much she was her father's child—in her dreams, her passion, her imaginative gifts.

Once they had moved to Long Island they saw "the children" infrequently. Occasionally some of them would drive out from the city to see their father. Sometimes they would bring a picnic and have it on the beach. Occasionally they may have been invited to dinner; if so, they did not stay. In any case, it was clear that their welcome was aloof.

And what of the Child during these visits? She hovered. She hovered between the protective shelter of her mother and the inchoate longing to be included in the chattering crowd who called their father "Pop" and evoked a spontaneity in him she rarely saw. Once they asked her to go to the beach with them. She ran to ask her mother, but the answer was curt: "They don't want you," she said. And so she didn't go.

In the summer after the first grade she changed schools and for the first time came into direct and daily contact with the environment of their select residential community. The school she now went to was experimental. There were no class rooms, no examinations. Just individual projects for which you had a tutor. For the Child it was in many ways a blissful experience. Her daydreams and fantasies were encouraged, and she was taught how to turn them into stories and poems. Words tumbled out of her and although she was so diffident in so much else, in this she was supremely sure. It was almost as though she had no need to be taught, as though there was some secret genie in her, a spirit that worked like magic. She won prizes; she received accolades; but that was not what mattered. What mattered was the surge of power and joy when the words would come in torrents and she would be enthralled by a force she did not understand.

But always, just below the surface, there was the nagging refrain that she did not really belong. There were no more than forty families in this village, but it was, in its own way, a "gold coast." Every family had its own tennis court, its own boats, its own stable. Most of them also had a nanny or a governess for its several children. As she grew older, the chasm between rich and poor grew deeper. Although she went riding with her classmates, she did not join them at the Hunt Club. Although she played tennis, her family did not belong to the Tennis Club. She was invited to their homes for lunches and parties but was seldom able to reciprocate. In addition she was a Catholic. On Saturday morning when the riding master took them for special lessons, she had to leave to go to catechism class. Her classmates were too well-mannered to comment but, even in their silence, she heard a jeer.

Strangely enough her humiliation and anger at being a Catholic did not color her sense of God. As long as she could remember, God had been part of her consciousness. Where this came from she did not know nor did she ever question. There was no need to question. What he was for her admitted no question. He was loving, compassionate, and understood her completely. If she was alien with the rest of the world, she was totally at ease with God. All the manmade rules of religion had nothing to do with God. He belonged to her without restraint. Commandments and regulations and the boring and bewildering questions and answers of the catechism had little to do with the God she trusted. It never occurred to her that God was in any way offended because she hated being a Catholic.

But the God of her heart was to be tested, for shortly after her twelfth birthday she was sent to a Catholic boarding school where her parents hoped she would learn more about being a Catholic. That fall was the first time she ever spoke to a Catholic child or a Catholic nun. Thus began four years of increasing alienation. For her there was no God in that place; he was crucified by rules and regulations, by suspicion and distrust. Students lied to their teachers and teachers tyrannized over their students. She lost all perspective. She often wanted to die. She was suffering, of course, from the blackness of depression, but such psychological problems were not admissible in those days. After all, young people had nothing to complain about. They had every reason to be happy.

One of her darkest memories was that of being questioned one night as she came upstairs to her dormitory. She had been taking a shower and she was late. As always a nun sat at the dormitory entrance, checking off her charges. "You're late." The statement offered no room for explanation and she gave none. A moment of silence and the nun said, "And you don't care, do you?" Silence again. "I wonder if there's anything you care about?" The question, so brutal, reached her heart. "No, Sister," she said with a smile she knew was more irritating than an argument. She went into her small cubicle and lay on her bed. The lights were already out. For hours she lay there unmoving, wondering in a kind of blank terror what would happen to someone for whom nothing in the world mattered—not even God.

By the time she was a senior she had given up all hope of love; she could neither give it nor accept it. She knew she would go to college and she wanted to go far away, where no one would know her, where nothing could touch her. Instead, at the age of sixteen she was registered against her will at the College of New Rochelle, a small liberal arts college for women, under the administration of the Ursuline nuns.

At the time it seemed like life's darkest revenge. She arrived angry (and, as always, frightened) and determined to hate everything she found. Her parents had promised her that when she was eighteen she could transfer to a college of her choice. But when the magic age came, she made no move. She had found classes exciting; she had made friends; she had regained the drive and ability to write. And contrary to all her intentions, she had begun to enjoy the nuns. She found them well-read, intelligent, amusing. They did not speak much about God, but in some intangible way it was clear that they lived for him. Most surprising of all, they seemed to love and enjoy one another.

By the time she received her BA degree, a transformation was in progress. God had found her again and this time he had brought her back from the bleak caves where she liked to hide into pastures where she was not alone. Slowly, the God of the Catholic faith was melded with her private God. By the time she graduated she had accepted (although warily) being a Catholic. Two years later she petitioned to be accepted as a postulant in the Ursuline Order.

When they learned her plans, her parents were wild with grief (her father) and anger (her mother). She was twenty-one years old, she had a BA degree with a major in English, and had worked for a year in a publishing house. Even more, she had been "going steady" for two years. To her parents her future looked very bright; but none of the possibilities they cited were enough to sway her. Her vocation was single-minded: to belong to God. That nuns lived in community, that Ursulines were teachers, that service and the desire to bring the Word of God to others, were an essential part of religious life simply never entered her consciousness. To belong to God—and to possess him as her own (private?) possession: that was as far as she could carry her vocation.

Thus I began my novitiate. The life of the novitiate was essentially a "private" life, characterized by silence and prayer. Sharing of any kind was not encouraged. Although there were conferences on community, on generosity, on service, basically the life itself fostered an individual quest for virtue (docility, obedience, humility) which translated into a quest for

God. Although there were hard times, I did not find the atmosphere hostile. I had lived away from home too long to be
homesick. Silence and aloneness had been an essential part
of my environment as long as I could remember. So I set out
with passion on my single-minded (con)quest for God.

The night before I was to make my temporary vows and
leave the novitiate was a night of terror. This quiet place had
nurtured me and offered me a home. To spend my life in
such a place did not seem like a hardship. Although I had
yearned for books, for music, for time to myself, this deprivation was nothing compared to my fear of returning to an environment in which I had so frequently felt alien and de-
spairing. The next years, I knew, would be spent in study and
teaching, and I feared them both.

My first assignment brought all my terrors into focus. The
first year I taught (without a day's preparation) sixty-two
first-grade girls in the local parochial school. The next two
years I was just as suddenly (and as ill-equipped) cast into
college teaching while getting a master's degree at a nearby
university. What startled me (and my superiors as well) was
that I was turning out to be very good at what I was doing.
By the time of my perpetual vows, my future ministry seemed
assured: I would teach English at the Ursuline college in New
Rochelle. With a few variations, this would be my life until
my eyes, my heart, or my mind gave out.

Once I proved my ability, my professional preparation began in earnest. In the summer of 1952, along with another
member of my community, I was sent to Washington to begin
my doctoral studies at the Catholic University of America. By
then I had completed several years of college teaching and many
of the courses, designed primarily for masters students, seemed
a waste of time. I had had an exalted idea of graduate study,
expecting my abilities to be taxed to the utmost; instead I often
found the work dreary and repetitive. Then, too, the attitude

of other nuns toward their studies disappointed me. They seemed far more interested in performing well in examinations than in expanding their horizons. I had expected something far less pragmatic. My effort to form a study group where we would discuss a literary work in depth petered out in favor of a session preparing for comprehensive examinations.

The Ursulines had no convent in Washington and for three years I lived in a student house at Sisters' College. It was during those years that I learned in practical terms what it meant to be an Ursuline. It was a far more profound learning experience than anything I learned in my courses. Other congregations, I recognized, while having far more external liberty, were far less free in their life of prayer. Many of them had meditation books which they were expected to follow; much of their prayer time was given to community vocal prayer. Ursulines, on the other hand, were encouraged to use the Gospels and were entirely free in the subject and the manner of our prayer. Prayer had been presented as the most important element in our day; never simply as an exercise to get through. The external freedom we sacrificed seemed a small price to pay for this spiritual ideal.

The dark side of the coin was that our family pride came close to arrogance. Because we were more monastic, because we had a more extensive life of prayer, because we were older in the Church (Saint Angela started her Company in 1535) we were inclined to presume a certain superiority. Looking back at those years, I am embarrassed at my unquestioned condescension and profoundly humbled by the unflagging kindness and generosity of the sisters I lived with. When I was too cloistered to take my shoes to be fixed, they graciously took them to the shoemaker. When our rules did not permit me to attend a simple ice-cream-and-cake birthday party, they came up to my room with a plate of goodies. It was not until many years later—in the renewal following

Vatican II—that I came to realize how far my attitude had been from the simplicity of Angela.

I finished my studies in 1958 and that fall resumed my life of teaching with renewed vigor and confidence. It is hard even now to sort out my reactions to those years. The last thing I would ever have expected to happen, happened: I became a very successful teacher. I developed, although not by design, a style, a rhetoric which was at once entertaining and acceptably academic. Perhaps it was my father's gift as a Celtic storyteller which emerged in me.

But this unexpected success was not enough to change my response to teaching: teaching remained a burden which at times was unendurable. I loved the preparation and the hours in the library, reading new material, preparing lectures and bibliographies. But the classroom! I dreaded walking into that room and seeing the door close behind me. No amount of success could dispel my reluctance. Although I outgrew my initial terror, the powerful disinclination remained. "Please don't make me do this; please don't make me talk, say things, engage in discussion," I prayed. "Please let me go and be alone." At times my reluctance diminished, and I walked in and out of classrooms as a matter of course. But the disinclination always returned, often bursting out more desperate than before. There were times when, without notifying the registrar or the dean, I simply walked into a classroom and wrote on the board "This class will not meet today" and went to my room and lay on my bed. Terror left me powerless. I could do no more.

Life at the college was, however, far more than teaching. Every able-bodied religious was pressed into service in the dormitories where each corridor had a presiding sister. Students in those days were, for the most part, responsive and appreciative, and although life in the dorms was physically and psychologically exhausting, it was also rewarding and energizing. Seeing adolescent girls mature into young women was a joyful process. Being able to help those with difficult problems was even more rewarding and watching them come to the fruition of graduation day was an experience of congratulatory joy.

Once again I discovered to my surprise that I was good at these tasks. I developed relationships with apparent ease, and acquired the reputation of being understanding, trustworthy, and faithful. As a result I rarely had a moment to myself. When I was not counseling students or preparing classes, I was engaged in the other multiple activities of the college.

Surely all of this was enough to occupy a life; but, in fact, this was only half our life. The religious context in which this ministry was exercised was even more demanding than the ministry itself. The Ursulines of the Roman Union, Eastern Province, USA prided themselves on scrupulous adherence to a monastic way of life dating back to seventeenth-century France. They observed strict cloister (exceptions: dentists, doctors, educational meetings). Their life of prayer rivaled that of contemplative orders: daily mass, one and a half hours of meditation, recitation of the Office, a half hour of spiritual reading, the rosary, two examinations of conscience, a visit of devotion to the Blessed Sacrament. Meals, of course, were eaten in silence. There were two periods of "recreation" daily after meals, although at least half the community was engaged in other work at these times. It was a form of life in which the superior (prioress) had complete power within the context of the Constitutions. The smallest digression from the Rule had to be ensured by a specific permission from her.

It was, perhaps, this tension between the major responsibilities of running an eminently successful college and the need for subjecting the slightest decision to a superior, who did not always understand the burdens of this exacting academic life, that frequently made life so onerous and frustrating.

But all of this is hindsight. At the time few of us realized the extent of the tension or acknowledged its causes. Perfection lay in never complaining. As a community we were far from unhappy. For the most part we loved our work, were well-prepared for it, and felt supported by our colleagues. We were a relatively young group, with energy, determination, confidence in our mission, and a wholehearted desire to give our lives to it. Those were years in which the college was eminently successful; we took pride in our achievement and in the achievements of our students—which in some way we claimed as our own. To be an Ursuline was an exalted vocation, and to be an Ursuline of the Roman Union was to reach the pinnacle. We were not far from a state of hubris.

What then was to be the response when the mountain came tumbling down and through the windows opened by Vatican II the soft wind of the Holy Spirit roared liked thunder? My recollection of those days is suspiciously vague. Could I have lived through such radical change and retained only such insubstantial memories? It would seem so. Part of this may be explained by the fact that I was clearly not the type for committee work or discussion groups and so managed to avoid a large segment of how our life was spent in those first years after the Council.

But more important than this was the fact that another facet of my life had opened before me. As early as 1949 the provincial had asked me to prepare a pamphlet on one of the famous Ursuline missionaries—Marie de l'Incarnation, who had come to Canada in 1639. I was overjoyed at the prospect because it gave back to me my first love: to be a writer. Although my other assignments continued unabated, I managed to keep on with the work—-snatching time from vacations, holidays, and an occasional free evening. The pamphlet grew into a book and in 1963 it was finished. Hopelessly naive, I sent it unrequested to the religious department of

Doubleday. Two weeks later I received a letter saying it was accepted for publication. The joy was too much for me and, without telling a soul of my triumph, I took to my bed with a violent headache. All the recommendations of Vatican II were as nothing compared to the possibility that I might, after all the desert years, become a writer.

But, of course, Vatican II did touch my life. Slowly we slid from the elegant constraints of our religious habits to an awkward garment we called a "modified habit." From there came experiments in dress: some colors approved as religious (gray, navy, blue, tan) and others condemned as "worldly" (burgundy, green, rose). These foolish distinctions were a classic example of how muddled and naive many of those early decisions were.

Cloister, too, was modified and the long hours of prayer, while not appreciably reduced, were more sensibly arranged. The most divisive change came in our response to community. Two of our communities numbered almost ninety sisters—clearly an unwieldy number for the collegial spirit recommended. Small communities grew up—some on the campus grounds, others in nearby apartments or small houses. In time we withdrew from life in the dormitories and set about the thorny task of learning to live together with the burdens of "ordinary life" (cooking, shopping, cleaning, and so forth). These were the years we said good-bye to many of our members—to some because they could not absorb the rapid changes; to others because the changes were not rapid enough.

Meanwhile I had written a second book—a biography of Henri IV of France. With my new freedom I had gone to the Library of Congress and the Widener Library at Harvard to do my research. In those days, like many university towns, Cambridge was teeming with antiwar protests, flower children, and psychedelic drugs. It also had its complement of religious—suddenly sprung from their convents and semi-

naries and in many cases working through a (very) late adolescence. *Relationship* was the word of the hour—and it came
in multiple varieties. Most of us escaped unharmed (and the
better for the experience), but there was a full share of disas-
ters: hasty intimacy, followed by hasty marriage, often end-
ing in bitter and bewildering divorce.

These two movements—a reduced teaching schedule
which gave me time to write professionally and the trend toward small-community living—changed my life dramatically.
The first moved me into a realm where I found myself whole,
complete, harmonious; the second came close to destroying
me.

I had no native abilities to cope with small-group living. I
was the single child of older parents and I had, to all intents
and purposes, been the product of boarding schools since the
age of twelve. I had adapted to institutional living with its
quiet, its privacy, its essential solitude. In my mind I recognized the values that were preached in the wake of Vatican II.
I applauded a more personal style of community, I applauded
the call to personal responsibility, to areas for free discussion,
for less ritualized prayer, for Gospel sharing.

Because it all seemed "the thing to do," I did it, casting
my vote for whatever was free, democratic, experimental. I
aped my peers and cheered the theology that affirmed that
God was everywhere: in our work, our celebrations, one another. The old spirituality which sought God only in private
prayer or the formalities of liturgy gave way to a new spirituality which was affirmed as more real, more human—and more
true.

This was the language that swirled around me and which
I accepted with the absolutism so much a part of my temperament. My hours of private morning prayer diminished
so that I could get to work earlier (after all, God was in my
work); Office often went unsaid in favor of watching a "con-

temporary" movie; spiritual reading was replaced by "sharing." While my peers seemed to be swimming into clear waters, I sensed the dangerous tug of a whirlpool. I was losing
my footing. The waters were closing over my head. The next
step was drowning.

I'm not sure when I realized this, but I think it was shortly
after one of the sisters in our small-community apartment
died of cancer. She had been sick off and on for two years.
For the two of us who lived with her during her final illness,
these were months of anguished uncertainty. She herself was
undemanding. She was not confined to bed. She was often
able to be about, even to drive to the beach, to enjoy a drink
and a good supper. But every hour held out to us the specter
of uncertainty. Our main convent had an infirmary, but this,
we knew without saying, would be unacceptable to her. She
was an intensely private person. She needed not an institution but a home where her two sister-friends would take care
of her without question. In the end she died very quickly,
after only thirty-six hours in the local hospital.

It was the end of September when she died, and there
were the first dark intimations of winter. I lived haunted in
those next months—not so much by death as by the need to
live fully, to keep the end in sight, and to shape one's life to it.
In this new perspective, the preceding years, with all their
activity, looked very empty.

The following spring the lease on our apartment expired
and our experiment in small-group living ended. It was when
I started to make decisions for my future that I realized how
rootless I had become. The decision to ask permission to live
alone for a few years came so immediately that I have never
been able to explain it. Nor is it easy to explain how unques-
tioningly the permission was granted.

Thus began a three-year pilgrimage. Once again I was on
a quest—this time not so much for God as for myself—al-

though I'm not sure that's a valid distinction. The two rooms I had on the third floor of a private house satisfied my need to live frugally. The "kitchen" was a makeshift alcove without either stove or running water. A two-burner gas stove sufficed for cooking and the bathroom (only a few feet away) sufficed for water. Although I was still teaching at the college and writing another biography, I now had the privacy to try to grope toward a life of prayer consonant with my temperament.

I lived hard in that first year, but it was not enough. I needed to live closer to the bone, although I was not even sure what that entailed. In the next two years, I visited two solitude communities for long periods of prayer—sandwiched in between my teaching. At Sarita, a hermit community on the King Ranch near Brownsville, Texas, I found myself. The need to apologize for what I was dropped away. To be slow, silent, reflective, a minimalist in many ways, was affirmed. "What are you so afraid of?" a resident hermit-monk asked me. "Of not being like everyone else." "Can you?" he pursued. I could only shake my head. I had tried; God knows I had tried. "So?" he shrugged his shoulders. It was the simplest of exchanges, but in his laconic style he had turned a key. When I returned to my attic apartment in New Rochelle it was in a new spirit of freedom. A few months later I moved back to our college community, my own identity sufficiently secure to enable me to be part of a larger whole.

Four years later I initiated a radical change in my life. My teaching career no longer seemed on track. For the first time in my life, I found myself at war with my students. Most of my courses were writing courses—short story, poetry, advanced essay. But the caliber of student was changing dramatically. The demands of my courses were beyond their abilities and yet I could not in conscience give them the grades they thought they deserved. I sympathized with them because it was not their fault that they were so poorly prepared, but I could not justify lowering the standards of the college.

I was fifty-nine years old—too young for retirement and yet increasingly dissatisfied with my academic life. I was also in difficulty with my writing. I had just completed a novel about religious life but despite the applause of my agent, the novel was not finding a publisher. I was in good health, energetic, experienced, well-educated. I certainly did not want to spend the rest of my life as a disgruntled religious. If I was to make a significant change, I knew that this was the time to do it. A few more years and it might be too late.

In such a mood I wrote to our central government in Rome, volunteering for overseas service. I made the areas of my service very clear: I was a university teacher in the field of English and American literature. In the back of my head, I think I had in mind a nice job in an Australian college where the climate was good and everyone spoke English. I wanted to be generous—but only within the bounds of reason.

The handwritten letter which reached me less than a month later had nothing reasonable about it. My qualifications would best be used, it read, in our Chinese mission college in Taiwan. Such a suggestion was too outlandish even to consider, and I put the letter in my pocket and went in to dinner. But, of course, it had to be considered. Why would I say no? Because it was a Chinese community into which I would never fit? because I knew no Mandarin? because it would be desperately lonely? For days I kept the letter under a pile in my desk, mentioning it to no one. When finally I read it to a friend, it had taken on a different tone—time had tamed the request. I could take it out now and talk about it, not as an idiotic suggestion but as a viable option.

The following month I spent my Easter vacation making a retreat of election at Maryknoll—the choice of place already predetermined my answer. Five months later I was in

Kennedy Airport waiting to board a flight for Korea and then on to Taiwan. The plane did not leave until midnight so I had all day to tidy up last-minute things and say a hundred good-byes. In retrospect my emotions during that day were very much like those I had experienced when entering the novitiate. There was, of course, the fear of the unknown, the fear one had aimed too high, that one simply didn't have the "right stuff." There was the terror, too, of the little things: how would I manage those eighteen cramped hours on the plane? What would happen to me in Seoul where I had a ten-hour layover? Would the directions be sufficiently clear so that I could find my plane to Taipei? And if I did not, what would happen to me in the mysterious and perilous East?

But below the fears was that powerful impulse which had originally led me to religious life and which was now leading me again: the impulse to give it all, to divest oneself of the known, the comforting, the human play of love. I wanted to be stripped bare of every security. My spirituality dictated that the less I had of everything, the more I would have of God.

I was sixty years old; I should have known better. After so many years my aspiration was still, "God alone." I was still unable to grasp that God did not exist, self-contained, in a barren universe. I know now, some fifteen years later, that this will always be my seduction: to see God as far off, silent and distant, living in inaccessible light—and, of course, supremely desirable. To be brought into the presence of such a God is worth any sacrifice. Although I recognize that with the coming of Jesus we have moved into an Incarnational spirituality, I also recognize that without an extraordinary grace I will never feel totally at ease in such a spirituality. It is something I must persistently work at and pray for.

As I grow older I realize more and more the impact of our early years on everything we become. My image of God, it

seems to me, comes not so much from my early religious education (of which there was very little) but from my own sense
of feeling alien, of feeling that I would never find a place in
the world. What more comforting for such a child than to
image a God who himself had so little to do with this world
but who lived in immense light and beauty, in a far-off realm
to which—if the child tries hard enough—she will find her
way. When I was very small, probably three or four, I would
occasionally have an experience which made me blissfully
happy. I would always be alone when it happened and then it
seemed to me that I would grow smaller and smaller, littler
even than my dolls, and this tiny creature that I was would be
enveloped in light, in a sphere of love, so bright, so penetrat-
ing that I never wanted it to end. Sometimes my mother would
find me and give me a shake and ask me what I was doing. I
could find no answer except to say, "I closed my eyes and I
got very small."

Whatever that experience was I don't know and there is
no reason to identify it. I do know, however, that it has had
a powerful impact on my life. To become very small in the
blissful immensity of God's light is for me an image of pure
love.

My years in Taiwan were salvific in many ways. I learned
in a new way that life is never a desert no matter how determined we are to make it one. There is always life, obscure
perhaps but greenly present. One finds one's level. Although
I had done my best to "leave everything behind," it was not
long before I found that my room was filling with books,
with a comfortable pillow, with a mug and some instant coffee. Against all my determination, I was finding my level.
And there was, of course, both love and laughter. I loved my
students; they amused me and I amused them. The myth of
the "inscrutable Oriental" was soon dispelled. These were
hard-wording, fun-loving young women with quick and

spontaneous bursts of laughter. Except for a few members of the community, all the sisters spoke some English, and although they did not enjoy it, they generously spoke it with me. My desert was soon filled. I was beginning to understand that famous Zen saying: Before enlightenment, I draw water and chop wood; after enlightenment, I draw water and chop wood.

After two years I returned to the United States. I thought it would be a simple matter to come home again. In fact, it was almost as difficult as my departure. I had not realized how completely I had tuned myself to another lifestyle. While I was in Taiwan, the novel I had had so much difficulty with had found a publisher and was doing well. It was time, I thought, for me to accept early retirement from the college and settle in to write full time. At last I had in my hands my lifelong dream: a life of quiet writing and research.

Instead my dream became my desert. Suddenly cut off from a very active life, I found the hours alone at my desk unendurable. I started another novel but could not move it along. I had always affirmed that if you worked hard enough, you could succeed. Inspiration, I had maintained, had nothing to do with it. But now, despite my efforts, I could not hit my stride. Meanwhile, I was contracted to translate a portion of the letters and memoirs of Marie de l'Incarnation from French to English. Although I loved the subject, the work of translation was tedious and unrewarding.

For several years I struggled along, ashamed of my apparent inactivity, angry at my inability to write productively, and bitterly regretting that I had left my career as a teacher. If it was a desert I had been looking for, I had surely found it! In time, however, small projects appeared on the horizon, and I leaped upon them. Little by little I found myself busy with various pieces of writing, with some lecturing, and a new love: archives.

The desert years were over as inexplicably as they had be-gun. Suddenly I was flooded with work, work that I loved, that energized me, that I felt was valuable, and that I was competent to do. "Grow old with me, the best is yet to be," wrote Omar Khayyám in his *Rubáiyát*. I could never have believed it until it became my experience.

In the end-time God has brought me along a straight path. The cliff's edge is still there but not under my feet. There are days, of course, when I still hide myself lest the "real me" be discovered. But on a normal day I can walk about the uni-verse with confidence. I take a staff to keep me steady. I look over my shoulder a little more than most perhaps. But you could say that I have become a "citizen of the world." For everything is mine and I am Christ's and Christ is God's.

Stick to Your Guns

Sharon Sullivan, OSU

Before I formed you in the womb I knew you, before you were born I dedicated you.

—Jeremiah 1:5a

My family loves a good argument, so much so that Sunday mornings after church would often find us gathered around the kitchen table in a heated discussion of the sermon, the Sunday school lesson, or some spin-off topic. The four of us—my brothers, my sister, and me, plus Mom at times—would battle away. Dad usually moderated, but left the point and the counterpoint to us combatants. It was as if he hoped we would emerge bloodied but unbowed in our convictions. When one of us started to give in to the others' arguments, Dad would demand, "Stick to your guns! If you have something to say, say it. If you believe it's true, convince us. Don't let us talk you out of it. Don't be easily dissuaded." He would later add, "Just be sure that what you say is true for you. That's all that matters. You may stand alone, you may be unpopular. But you'll be true to yourself."

This was Dad's credo, and I accepted it as truth, as children often do, assuming that all families operated out of the same belief. It was my mom who would remind me, "Your daddy may say 'stick to your guns,' but remember, the harder part is finding out just exactly what is true for you and why." I would discover how right she was. These two elements—

the commitment and the search—became the benchmarks for my own faith journey. Perhaps they help account for how this Texas Baptist baby emerged, much later in life, as an Ursuline Sister of Maple Mount, Kentucky—or as my Texas relatives would say, "a Roman Catholic nun."

As members of University Boulevard Baptist Church in Houston, Texas, "going to church" was an accepted part of life. We went to Sunday school and worship service, and on Sunday nights I attended something called "Rainbows." I learned about God's love, sang "This Little Light of Mine" and "Jesus Loves Me," and played in a rhythm band that occasionally gave concerts to the whole church. There was only one set of cymbals, so I got to be the director.

But the day came—I was four or five years old—when my parents said that we were moving to another church; we were going on a "treasure hunt" for a church that would be just right for us. This treasure hunt is my earliest memory of being truly aware of what *search* and *commitment* might mean for us as a family.

We searched for nearly two years—Methodist, Lutheran, Christian, Episcopalian, Presbyterian—attending a certain church for perhaps two months, sometimes only one Sunday. I heard again and again about the same "Jesus," and from that experience came to believe that while there appears to be only one God, there are many ways to express faith and to worship. I learned that it was each person's duty and privilege to discover that expression for herself. Even at the tender age of seven, I knew this to be a basic truth for me.

Our treasure hunt for a church also made me aware of my family's rather ecumenical—or confused, depending upon one's perspective—background. Dad was a Texas Baptist, Mom was Episcopalian, but her mother was Lutheran; my sister, Shelby, had been baptized Episcopalian because she was born during the War while my dad was overseas. When I was born, my dad was back home, and we were a Baptist family again.

Baptists did not accept infant baptism, so I grew up a heathen child among a family of the baptized. When we ended our search for a faith family at Bellaire Presbyterian Church, I was the only six-year-old in the Sunday school class who had not been baptized. While this fact gave me a little notoriety, it also troubled me, for I felt that I was somehow left out of the full life of the community.

Since Presbyterians *do* believe in infant baptism, my brother, Rob, born later that year, was ready to be baptized in the fall. When Mom asked me if I would like to be baptized with Rob, she had no idea how excited I would become. At last, at the age of seven, I would become a full member of the Church—or so I thought.

The minister took our family into a tiny room, sprinkled water on Rob's head, and asked my parents if they would promise to bring him up in a Christian home. Then the minister brought the water to me and baptized me "in the name of the Father, Son, and Holy Ghost." Instead of turning to my mom and dad with his questions, however, he asked *me*: "Do you believe in God? Will you promise to follow Jesus?"

Well! I was an eager and solemn-eyed seven-year-old, dressed in my best black patent leather shoes and ruffled socks (what agony!), and had been waiting for this moment for a long, long time. What else could I say? "Yes!"

At that moment, God had me, and years later that moment would be a steady beacon of light in times of darkness. I was baptized. I belonged to God. I was home. I was a child of God, a member of a universal family. That knowledge became another piece in my puzzle of truth.

In the Presbyterian tradition, the Lord's Supper—Holy Communion—occurred regularly every three months plus Christmas and Easter. Although I had seen this sacrament only half a dozen times, and although I was not allowed to participate, it had somehow become the pivotal moment of worship for me, the key to my faith. I had convinced myself that as a baptized member of Bellaire Presbyterian Church, I would finally get to take part in the Lord's Supper.

I met with disappointment, however. Yes, I was a child of God; sure, I was baptized; yes, I was a member of the community. But according to the rules, I was not old enough to appreciate the meaning of the Lord's Supper. I had to wait three years, until I was older.

The three years passed. Then, just as I was about to begin the communicants' class (for those preparing for Holy Communion and full participation in the Church), it was moved to an older grade, and I missed out. When I finally reached the appropriate age to participate in the communicants' class, my family moved to Kentucky—and again I missed out. In Owensboro, Kentucky, the First Presbyterian Church had already completed their communicants' class, meaning that, once again, I missed out. By then, I was thirteen years old. When the next communicants' class began, nothing was going to keep me from participating.

Imagine my amazement when we began to study the "meaning of the Lord's Supper," and I discovered that Presbyterians believe the bread and wine are merely symbols of an event, that participation in the Lord's Supper is a memorial act only. Presbyterians, according to our instructor, Mr. Laufer, believe in something called "consubstantiation," and that what I said I believed was "transubstantiation," which is what Catholics believe. I was staggered, for I knew what was truth for me: the bread and grape juice were somehow truly Jesus.

I was torn. I could stick to my guns and believe what was true for me, or I could hold my tongue and complete the communicants' class. I held my tongue and became a full Presbyterian communicant.

As I grew older, I became a committed and involved Presbyterian. I participated in the youth group, Sunday school, youth synod, choir, church camp, vacation Bible school. I studied, learned, and discussed, and became very comfortable being a Presbyterian who enjoyed a satisfying relationship with God. But I remained alert, searching for others who might understand the truth I knew about the Lord's Supper, those who could help me understand more fully what such a mystery meant and required.

In the next twenty years, three more truths would become my own and would govern my life: God loved the world into being and is doing so today; God demands total surrender of each of us; only through God's love are we empowered in all things. My understanding of these truths drew me inexorably toward the Catholic Church, and later to the Ursuline Sisters of Maple Mount, Kentucky.

Because singing was—and remains—a treasured element of Presbyterian worship, it is no surprise that a large part of my theological understanding was formed from the words of Presbyterian (and Baptist) hymns. I remember singing two or three hymns in Sunday School, followed by three or four more during worship service. Of course we sang the favorites over and over—all the verses, followed by a hearty "Amen." Such was our enthusiasm that the choir, the organist, and the congregation often ended up in a heated race to see who could finish first. But the words and the emotions that the hymns evoked entered, remained, and formed a portion of my spirit.

An early—and still—favorite was "For the Beauty of the Earth." I often sang the words of this song as I watched a Texas blue norther sweep in from the northwest, or when Shelby and I played games with the thunder and lightning of a hurricane in the Gulf off Galveston…and then laid awake at night mesmerized by the storm. It was almost impossible to watch the wind play in the grass, to marvel at the first fig ripening on our tree, to study a snake among the blackberry brambles, and not be awestruck by the overwhelming and almost tangible presence of God. I used to take a book with me and climb the chinaberry tree in our back yard (we had cottonwoods too, but Dad said they were too brittle to climb). Leaving the book unread, I would perch among the branches lost in fascination with the veins on the leaves, the bugs crawling on the twigs, or the clouds tumbling overhead. I don't know that those times were conscious prayer, but I believed them to be privileged and intimate moments with my God.

In "Ode to Joy," we sang of "field and forest, vale and mountain," but Houston doesn't really have forests and vales and mountains, and I didn't have glasses until we moved to Kentucky, so I couldn't really see the stars. Once there, however, surrounded by the woods, valleys, hills, mountains, and clear autumn nights, I let these words become my mantra. As I grew older and became involved in Girl Scouts, I found an open and comfortable fellowship in which to share these rich experiences of faith.

Just south of Owensboro, in a perfect jewel of a setting—woods, hills, hidden valleys, rocks, and a deep clear lake—was the Pennyroyal Girl Scout Camp. That and other regional scout camps became my second home. I explored and created trails, learned woodcraft, absorbed music, and talked: talked, talked, talked, with other scouts. Our conversations—

enjoyed by both Catholics and Protestants—often turned to what today would be called "faith sharing." Faith, not dogma, was the focus.

"Scout's Own" is an integral event in any scout camping experience. During a Scout's Own, each girl is encouraged to spend a little time reflecting on poetry, song, Scripture, or silence, with nature and service to others as common themes. At these times, often on a small wooded knoll that overlooked the Camp Pennyroyal lake, I came to know my God in the beauties of nature. I also grew to appreciate that others shared my love affair with the natural world and with its Creator.

Years later I introduced other young scouts to the richness and solace of nature. Girls from the inner city often came to Pennyroyal, unsure of themselves and afraid of anything with more legs than they had. By the end of their experience, however, they would be capturing multilegged hairy crawlers for me to name or exclaim over, and proudly displaying them for everyone else to see. What a chance that was for me to see God in their faces, as well as in those hairy critters, and to marvel at the power of God's gentle love.

When I was in my mid to late twenties, I worked several summers at Camp KYSOC, an Easter Seal camp for "mentally and/or physically handicapped children and/or adults." (At that time political correctness was not an issue.) We counselors often wondered who were the people with the "handicaps"—the campers or the counselors. It was there that I was challenged and led to understand yet another dimension of God and nature.

Joanne, one of the campers—who became my friend and mentor—had quadriplegic cerebral palsy; she was wheelchair-bound and could move only her head. Throughout most of the day Joanne would be isolated in her chair, unable to initiate any physical interaction. But every afternoon Joanne would ask us to free her from the wheelchair and lay her on the ground. We would spread a blanket for her, to soften the twigs and other debris beneath the trees, but she wanted to have at least her bare feet on the ground itself. Once she was settled, Joanne would relax her neck and head, sigh from the depths of her soul, close her eyes, and murmur, "Now I am connected; I will draw power and rest."

In touch with the ground, Joanne felt completely alive, as though she were being plugged into a recharger. Although these sessions often held moments of high humor, they almost always became occasions of prayer. She saw God's creation—all of it—as dynamic, demanding a dynamic response. In my own way, I had been praising God for the marvelous show, but had almost missed God's active nurturing love in the world about me.

From that time on, my love of all the earth as creation and creature, and my commitment to its protection and regeneration, took on new depth and strength. Later I would find within the Maple Mount Ursulines of Mount Saint Joseph an echo of that connectedness with the land and union with the earth.

Writing of my relation with God as Lover of Creation is not difficult, but writing of my struggle with the God of Surrender is much harder to articulate. I am reminded of the "altar call" that is often a part of worship in many faith traditions. This is a moment of great joy and deep sorrow, when those who so desire approach the altar to surrender their lives to God.

As those who choose to answer the call move toward the altar, the rest of the congregation sings these or similar words: "Just as I am without one plea..."

These words, with their recognition of individual helplessness and hint of approaching God empty-handed, imply "total surrender to God." In Sunday school and college jam sessions we avoided the harder questions about what this "surrender" truly involved, and talked instead about "dedicating our life to God" or "giving our whole heart to God." Somehow these terms seemed to suggest that we would be doing God a favor—or at least be engaging in a partnership of some kind with God.

At the time, my relationship with God was a friendly matter that I controlled—a control I did not want to give up. When I was sixteen I toyed with the idea of becoming a minister or missionary, but decided that was a little more "total" than God wanted from me—or than I was willing to give to God.

I began my college career as a Trustees' Scholar with a full scholarship to Christian College, a two-year women's college in Columbia, Missouri. It was not exactly my first preference, but with all my expenses completely paid, it seemed the wiser choice. I was a math major until there were no more courses for me to take. Then I became an English major and graduated with honors, completing a history project on "Andy Jackson and the Labor Unions." (My dad was an economic conservative, so I never shared that paper with him.)

I then went to Maryville College, a Presbyterian college in Maryville, Tennessee, in the foothills of the Smoky Mountains. It was an age/era/time of political activism, and we student "radicals," certain that we were making a cynical but telling observation, delighted in referring to Maryville as a "small Christian college for small Christians."

At Maryville, I switched majors again, from English to history. I believed that true seekers of wisdom had to suffer in the process. The study of math and English had been painless for me; I thought that studying history might let me suffer and thus lead me to wisdom. Surprisingly, I enjoyed history and gained some wisdom in spite of the lack of suffering.

Although I obviously struggled with choosing an appropriate major, I firmly believed I was in control of my life and was managing my relationship with God quite well, thank you. God was around when I prayed, sort of a "dial-a-God." God's and my discussions were intellectual and well-ordered and generally covered such issues as the Democratic National Convention, Vietnam, Martin Luther King, Jr., and pollution. Oh, yes, I was troubled in the heart by the wretched conditions I saw when I volunteered as a tutor and recreation leader with the Presbyterian mission at Home Avenue in Maryville, a settlement of low-income families and a hotbed of the Ku Klux Klan, moonshine whiskey, and abusive and dysfunctional families. And perhaps I chastised God about children born with crippling conditions, especially those I had encountered while working with Campus Girl Scouts at Christian College. But I rarely got beyond my comfortable, well-reasoned, intellectual relationship with God. I could line up my truths, assess how well I was "sticking to my guns," and return to my dorm room satisfied and a little smug.

One day in November 1968, in a dormitory room in Columbia, where I had returned to visit my first alma mater, this orientation came to an end. I had joined a discussion with other aluma, and as the night turned toward morning, we searched more deeply into what it meant to be Christian—a child of God. As I sat on the double bed and spoke to the group with great clarity of my well-ordered and reciprocal relationship with God, Sally Appel reached over and put her hand on my arm. "But Sharon," she said, "that can't be all; God wants *all* of you." "But he has me," I insisted. "No; you have only let him share your head. You must surrender your entire self and will into God's hands. That is the only way you can ever become fully free."

I did not want to hear any more about such surrender, and I virtually ran from the room, rushing from the truth that followed. In my heart of hearts, I was an independent Texan-cum-Kentuckian, a Presbyterian, and a pal of God. But in no way was I going to become a *slave* of God; I would not give up my cherished freedom, my individuality. Besides, God did not want that from me.

But Sally was right, and I was terrified. I fumed and fretted over the surrender discussion on the plane back to Maryville, in classes as I tried to take notes, during walks in the college woods, at home for Christmas vacation. I was haunted by that conversation and the knowledge that Sally was right. I read Peter Marshall, poetry, Lloyd C. Douglas, Scripture, Catherine Marshall, hymns—and Sally remained right. I was simply afraid of the very idea of surrender; I was plagued by doubts and fears of my own making. What if I surrendered all of me and never found myself again? Worse, what if I surrendered myself to this God I thought I knew, and there was no one there? Worst of all—the greatest fear: what if I got up the nerve to surrender, and God did not want me after all. These fears were wide of the mark and actually reflected my own doubt that I simply would not be able to do this thing call "surrender."

Back at Maryville, as it snowed in the mountains that third week in January, I wandered the college woods consumed by tears. But when the dark night had passed, my surrender was complete; effected not by me, but by God. At the time I thought it was "once for all," but of course time and again the surrender has come in tears and sighs. For that twenty-one-year-old college senior, however, it was a moment of ultimate truth.

I did not know what to do with myself; the whole world had somehow subtly changed, and I had changed with it. My ears strained to hear the voice of the Lord and Ruler of my heart, my life; anything could have happened and I would not have been surprised. And it did.

On the night of January 25, I was in charge of the dorm, as senior resident advisor, because our "dorm mother" was in the hospital. Anne, one of the student residents, came in at midnight, visibly upset. I followed her to be sure she was all right, and found her sitting in the hall pounding on her leg with the point of a knitting needle. When I touched her shoulder, she bolted from the chair, ran past me, and flung herself out on the balcony. I pursued her into the freezing night (barefoot and in cut-offs).

Anne stood on the railing of the balcony looking down at a drop of over thirty feet. "Oh, my God," I prayed—a prayer of my whole being—"help me." Anne was inconsolable, rigid, terrified, and restless. With her arms folded against her breasts, she paced back and forth on the five-inch railing.

"You know," I gently observed, "I can never find the Big Dipper in January." I prayed again: "My God, help me." Anne stopped her pacing but remained standing on the railing. As she glanced up at the stars, we began to talk. I do not remember what we said, but I certainly remember my desperation, for Anne could not be consoled. The longer we talked, the more my prayer became: "Not me, God, but you."

Later I was told that we were out there for over two hours, in below-freezing temperatures, but time had ceased to have meaning in those hours. Eventually, Anne's restlessness returned, and she resumed her pacing along the railing. I paced below her, on the balcony, afraid to reach up toward her lest she fall. Finally she stopped and stared out over the campus. "God, God," I prayed, "I can do nothing. Take my hand," and at that moment, Anne slipped and started falling over the edge of the railing. As her hand flew up, mine shot out— and I pulled her back from the fall and onto the balcony. There was no human way I could have done that; she was already fully falling—yet, we fell to the balcony together in a heap.

As I held her, I repeatedly crooned above her sobs, "It was God's love, Anne, only God's love," a prayer of both gratitude and praise. I had never known such power of God. But the promise had been there all along—from Sally, in Paul, from Jesus—that only in total surrender can God work through us. I was shaken, overwhelmed, and primed for the next step.

When Anne finally slept, I sat and watched and waited for the morning. I can't remember what we did with Anne, but as soon as the light broke, I went to see the chaplain, a Presbyterian minister who lived on the Maryville College campus with his family. I simply wanted someone to help me understand what was happening in my soul. All that "breaking in" of God in an otherwise well-ordered life was unnerving. But he could not help; he could not even hear me. I went away confused and frightened. Something had happened in the night and in the week before; I knew that something was required of me—and I was not sure I wanted any of it. I swung from high to low, and ran from Anne and from God.

Several weeks later a group of Medical Mission Sisters came to campus for an extended weekend to sing, evangelize, and otherwise hobnob with the students. Since they stayed in my dorm (I was still substitute dorm mother) I had to make all the arrangements. I had never really seen a nun, except for *The Sound of Music* and *The Flying Nun*, so I didn't know what they needed, how to talk to them, how to act. Still reeling from the past weeks' encounters with God, this seemed like yet another intrusion. But I, along with most of the campus, was captivated by these Medical Mission Sisters. They were gentle, energetic, and quite real; they were playful and adventuresome. When they wanted to hike in the Smoky Mountains and had nothing appropriate to wear—

just recently out of the habit—we borrowed hiking clothes for them: boots, sweatshirts, hats, scarves, pants. The Sisters joined in with great humor through it all, endearing themselves to us even more.

While they were there, the Sisters rehearsed their music in one of the dorm rooms, and I sat and listened for hours. Sister Lucy Whelan seemed to sense that I was troubled and encouraged me to talk. She listened to my story, and in the listening brought me peace. I was not going crazy; something had occurred. No doubt God would make it clearer.

I was intrigued by Sister Lucy's gentleness, peace, and total commitment to God—not that I thought God might have something like that in store for me. After all, I was a Presbyterian—more or less. Then, at a farewell pizza dinner, just before the Sisters left, I found out that Sister Lucy was a convert. Amazing! You didn't have to be born a Catholic to become a nun! I hadn't known such a thing was possible. I wasn't "safe" after all!

The nagging image of me as some kind of nun haunted my mind for weeks after the Medical Mission Sisters left, so I wrote of my dilemma to Sister Lucy. A few months later her reply came: "Keep listening to God," she encouraged. "You'll know if the call is for you. Remember, a vocation to follow God does not necessarily mean becoming a Catholic nun."

Whew! What a relief! I could put that weird thought out of my mind—and I did. I accepted as truth that God demanded total surrender, but I did not yet understood that most of my life would be a continual struggle to surrender to God.

For the next several years I tried to put the "God thing" behind me. I moved to Lexington, Kentucky, studied history in graduate school, and dropped out almost immediately to work full-time in accounting and bookkeeping. I made friends, explored the world of nature, remained politically active, made no major life decisions, and just enjoyed being alive.

One March day in 1971, I decided to quit my job and apply to work for the Girl Scouts. I was not sure why I decided to do that; I simply knew it was the right direction. I had no reason to think there was a job waiting for me, but in one corner of my heart I believed that God was prodding me to "get on with it." As things evolved, scouting was not my final destination, but it was definitely on the way.

With that decision at heart, I resigned my job the next day, visited the local Girl Scout office, and submitted my application. The executive director warned me that it would probably be at least six weeks before a position opened and that when it did, it might be anywhere. That sounded fine to me. I called Mom to let her know what I had done; she just chuckled.

The next day, the executive director of the Pennyroyal Girl Scout Council in Owensboro called to ask me to interview with them for an immediate job opening. Within the week I had an apartment in Owensboro and a job with the Pennyroyal Girl Scout Council. In no time, my days filled with the natural rhythm of recruiting scouts, developing programs, and teaching campcraft to the troop leaders. Was that God?

Within two months, however, this rhythm changed abruptly when my father had a massive and life-changing stroke, the first in a nine-year series. My brothers were still in high school, my sister was in Nashville, and I was—unbelievably—in Owensboro, ready to be a support for Mom. Was that God again? Was this the truth I must accept—that once we surrender, God continues asking for more and making it possible to give more? I began to believe it was so.

But I was only beginning to understand how surrender fashions a life of faith. While I had begun to accept the need for continued surrender to God, I had barely begun to understand the empowering nature of God's response. With Dad's first stroke a powerhouse of prayer sprang into action. Friends—Presbyterian, Episcopalian, Catholic—offered their prayer and support. Dad survived, but at great personal cost. Over the next nine years he would suffer recurring strokes of varying severity, with the last and most destructive occurring in 1981. Early in this period, Dad underwent open-heart bypass surgery, a relatively new and dangerous procedure at that time. During this time, my mom began her twenty-four-year odyssey (to date) with Parkinson's disease.

Although my parents continued to receive their encouragement and support from their friends and faith community, much of my support came from the Girl Scout community: a group of volunteers, scouts who attended Immaculate Catholic Church, and the Goetz family. These people saw my distress and opened their hearts and homes; when I needed a place to touch base and regain my equilibrium, they were there—with bratwurst, beer, and a caring ear and heart.

I was having a very hard time understanding just where this loving, empowering God fit in the picture of a dad who had been devastated almost beyond recognition and a mom who was losing her will day by day in a battle with Parkinson's and her fears for my dad. With her own reliance on God, Dee Goetz, who would later become my confirmation sponsor, helped me see God's empowering love: in Dad's determination to salvage some part of his life—even if it was only building a lopsided exercise corner in the basement—and in Mom's daily fidelity to sharing a moment of humor and setting that jaunty hat at precisely the right angle. There was a gentleness and open acceptance among the Goetzes, the young scouts, and the volunteer families—a gentleness and acceptance that clearly spoke of God's love. Not that the same spirit was not among the fine people in the Sunday school or on the education committee at First Presbyterian Church; I just could not see it there as easily. I was becoming restless with my questions—again.

Our Girl Scout camp was not accessible to girls who were physically challenged, and very little effort was made to include girls with mental disabilities. Both groups had been involved, to a certain extent, in other Girl Scout activities, but even these efforts were disappearing. Because one of my responsibilities with the Girl Scouts was to direct and help develop the camping programs, I wanted to resurrect these programs and make the camp more accessible.

When I presented the idea to the board of directors, they were not receptive; one member even worried aloud about "those people" burning down the camp. Angered, I resolved to learn more about "those people" and educate the board of directors and others like them. I began taking classes in special education at Brescia College, a local liberal arts college affiliated with the Ursuline Sisters.

Sister George Ann Cecil, head of the special education department, encouraged and expected her students to volunteer in a variety of programs for those with special needs; one of the most popular was Catholic religious education for children and adults with mental disabilities. I volunteered. Every other Saturday we would gather—college students and the adults and children with mental disabilities—to sing, pray, and revel in the love of God. There were no pretensions; every hug, every laugh, every exclamation of awe, every "gimme five," was from the heart. It was like receiving my own instructions in the true meaning of faith, surrender, and trust in the empowering love of God.

I gave up fighting. Encouraged by the Goetzes, by my Immaculate Church Girl Scout troop of seventh- and eighth-graders, and by the example of Sister George Ann's special people, I decided to see if I was brave enough to seek conversion to the Catholic Church. I had been a history major in college and had developed a love for the Renaissance and Reformation period; certainly I was not naive about the checkered history of the Church in the world. By the same token, I had come to believe in the incredible strength of the Church which, in spite of human failings and horrible abuses, had born witness to God's love for two thousand years. After reading *1001 Questions About the Catholic Church*, I realized that I had none of those questions, and that silly fears were all that were holding me back. So I took the plunge.

It took me nearly ten days to find the courage to drive from my apartment to the rectory at Saint Stephen's Church, about half a mile away. When finally I parked across the street from the rectory, it took me another half an hour and many detours to get to the front door. I convinced myself that if there was no light on, then that obviously meant that God didn't want me to go any further—but there was a light on. I walked around the rectory three times in the December cold, and again, convinced myself of God's participation—or lack of participation—in the whole thing: *I'll knock and if no one comes, then God doesn't want me to do this.* Poor God. When I finally knocked, the door opened immediately, almost as though Father Willett had been standing there waiting for me to get up my nerve.

I had never met the man; I did not know what I was doing; I was scared. "Hi!" I shouted. "What do you have to do to be a Catholic?" Father Willett smiled at me, ushered me in with a sweep of his arm, and said, "Why, you come on in and sit down." So, I did.

In 1972 and 1973, many post-Vatican II processes were still experimental; I don't even know if RCIA (Rite of Christian Initiation of Adults) existed. Father Willett and I decided that I would become a class of one, and we began immediately, finding readings and books that would challenge and edify me. When Father was temporarily transferred to a town sixty-five miles away, I packed a sack lunch and, between Girl Scout training sessions, took instructions sitting on his back porch with glasses of Seven-UP, watching the spring come in. Four months later, I was ready to be confirmed in the Catholic Church.

When I finally talked with my folks about my decision, Mom confided that she wished she had found the nerve to convert when she was younger; Dad was a little more hesitant. "Why can't you just be Episcopalian?" and "What if the pope says you can't have Protestant friends?" I put his fears to rest and assured him, "It's not like I'll become a nun or anything like that." "Well," he concluded, "just be a good Catholic, and don't hop from church to church." Like the dad of old, he gave me his blessing and told me to stick to my guns.

On April 26, 1973, with my parents in attendance along with my brother Rick, the Goetz family, and the members of my Girl Scout troop, I was confirmed by Father Willett instead of the bishop (another Vatican II experiment), and received my first Communion in the Catholic Church. When the Mass was over, we came spilling out of St. Stephen's in such high excitement that people passing on the street below asked, "Who got married?" My scouts kept saying to me, "Aren't you glad you met us?" They were so very proud of this gift of faith they had given me. At last God had empowered me to come home to my faith family; my truths to which I had clung and from which I had run were being affirmed. I should have been content—but in truth, my journey had just begun.

Over the next eight years I continued to grow and search—no longer for a faith home but for a better understanding of God's empowering love and what that meant in my life. As special education became more important to me than Girl Scouts, I once again became a volunteer and completed my teacher certification in regular education and special education.

Throughout that time I came into contact with more Maple Mount Ursulines of Mount Saint Joseph. There was Sister James Rita, who taught me that you can "always find something to praise in a student's work, even if it's just neat margins." There was Sister Clarita, who taught us to say "children's literature" instead of "kiddie lit." There was Sister Marty and Sister Kathy ("junior Sisters," a term I found quite funny at the time), who joined in whatever student activities were allowed them. A fellow student, Donna Goetz, and I hatched a dream in which we, along with Sister Marty and Sister Kathy would reopen a defunct Catholic parish school for a subsistence salary, live on the property, and be a "Christian witness" group. When we ran this by Sister James Rita, she said it was a laudable idea, but at this stage of their formation, Sister Marty and Sister Kathy needed a community experience. I was not really certain why Donna and I did not constitute a "community experience," but decided that an important part of being Ursuline (not that I wanted to be one) must include a life lived for God *in community*.

During those years I also learned more about the human variety of love. For example, it was impossible to spend a summer at Camp KYSOC and emerge unchanged. For thirteen weeks we would work among, with, and for people whose daily existence was often a heroic struggle, but who greeted each day as though it were a marvelous treat. We would tend to all the bodily needs of our campers—dressing, nursing, feeding, bathing; with great compassion, we learned to love those ravaged bodies and souls.

The entire experience was a growth in self-love as well. I came to understand that I, who so often ran in fear from God and from other "in-breaking" encounters, could love and be loved as a whole person. In time, I would understand that this was yet another evolving portion of my being that would respond to the call that was growing more insistent within. Still, I had to find a way to share that knowledge of God's empowering love.

Although I taught special education in the public schools, volunteered with the Red Cross and the Girl Scouts, tithed, participated in the life of the Church, and tried not to run too hard from God, I could not escape the sense that something more was required of me. Being with the scouts at camp and with the staff at KYSOC was always so life-giving. We were a group of people committed to the same goal of helping and enabling persons. But it was only for a summer or two, after which we would leave that supporting and committed community to return to our regular jobs—usually in some branch of the healing or helping professions. I considered joining the Peace Corps or volunteering for the missions in Point Barrow, Alaska, but those would only be a temporary commitment as well, and somehow too limited. It was becoming reluctantly clear to me that I was ready to consider accepting a lifetime commitment to *something* greater than my own vision. The old fear was growing again: Just what is up God's sleeve?

One question kept creeping into the corners of my mind and around the edges of my heart: *Could I ever be—do I think it's possible—could I become—an Ursuline Sister?* This question actually frightened me more than my earlier thoughts about daring to convert. But, like those goofy "8 balls" with the mystical messages that float to the surface, the notion kept reasserting itself: *Don't be ridiculous.* How could I join the ranks of such ladies as Sister James Rita and Sister George Ann? I wore blue jeans to teach, was happiest in overalls or cut-offs out in the woods or in a canoe, enjoyed a good knee-slapper, and cheered for the Dallas Cowboys. Surely I was totally unsuited for such a "holy life." (I had forgotten the group of Ursulines who stayed at the Girl Scout camp one freezing weekend in 1972, huddled around the fire, teaching us a card game called "Spit on Your Partner." Much later I would also learn that Sister James Rita craved black jelly beans and was addicted to the soap opera, *Dallas*.) I just knew that such a place, such a commitment, such a community, was not for me. *They* wouldn't want me, and I was fairly certain I wouldn't want them.

But reality—or God—kept breaking into my perceptions.

A Girl Scout friend who was a former Ursuline told hilarious tales of the Ursulines and Mount Saint Joseph that did not mesh with my "holy" image. Some of the Sisters at Brescia College (Sister Corda, who won a keg of beer, or Sister Elaine, who played a mean game of intramural volleyball and basketball) kept breaking the oh-so-pious image. Yet I hesitated to even voice the thought—for in my true and most private moments of prayer, I knew I was a broken, frightened, reluctant, and quite backward child of God. What on earth did I have to offer? Better just to slink off again before God spotted me.

I met an Ursuline Sister who was on a leave of absence as she struggled to discover the truth of her vocation. She seemed to be wrestling, in different ways, with many of the same questions that troubled me. As we became friends we would sit together after a day's work, sharing a cup of Lapsing Sushong tea, pondering imponderable questions. At times, I would listen to her and think, *How odd. We are both considering the same call, but one is deciding whether to leave and the other whether to come.*

I grew to understand much of my friend's brokenness, and to cherish that brokenness as part of her giftedness. In so doing, I began to accept some of my own brokenness and to believe that "broken" was okay for the Ursulines.

As things progressed, my friend returned to the Ursuline community, but our friendship remained. She continued to participate in Girl Scout functions and encouraged me to expand my involvement in the life of the Church by helping with youth ministry at a local parish where she worked. Although my searching and questioning continued, I hesitated to discuss it openly, lest it take on a life of its own.

Throughout the next few years I stutter-stepped toward a commitment and expanded my other horizons. Through my Girl Scout activity, I got involved with cross-country bicycling, learned to rappel cliffs, went spelunking in wild caves, and even jumped out of a plane a few times—with a parachute of course. I completed most of my master's course work, reconsidered the missions in Alaska, reworked some public school environmental education programs, and looked for ways to expand my community involvement. My apartment was a private library with bed and kitchen, my prayer life was again well-ordered, my brothers and sister were married, my social life and my need for privacy had reached a nice balance, and my parents were holding their own (or so it seemed). I believed all was right with my world, and hoped that this "nun thing" was just a fad. In an exercise in my class on abnormal psychology that fall, the professor asked us to indicate the two most likely scenarios for our lives in the next five years. When I wrote "nun or eighteen-wheel truck driver," and knew these choices to be true, I decided it was time to act.

Late in 1980, I began what would be a four-year pilgrimage through initial formation. I came to the Ursulines of Maple Mount—hospitable women, bonded to the land, educators, pioneers, committed witnesses of the empowering love of God—and they invited me to journey with them. During the "contact program," our first official step in formation, I continued my teaching, Girl Scout activity, and community involvement. In addition, I met more Ursulines, explored my call with a "contact Sister," and joined in daily morning prayer with the small Ursuline community at Ewing Court. Carrying all my teaching gear, I biked in my sweats to pray the Morning Office (a new experience), and then biked the seven miles to Sutherland Elementary School where I was teaching. I was conditioning myself for a transcontinental bike trip—sort of a last fling before the nunnery.

After half a year in the contact program, I made formal application to the community, took a battery of tests that included questions like "Does it bother you if someone spits on the sidewalk?" and "Do you have visions?" I met the five other applicants—the eldest of whom would soon turn twenty-one.

As I waited for the community's response, sewed pockets into a couple of skirts, and made my final preparations for the bike trip, my dad had his final massive stroke. Although we were certain he would not make it, he walked out of the hospital less than ten days later. I had thought the other strokes had devastated my dad, but that one was the worst. He had become "emotionally labile," which meant he no longer could control or depend upon a reasonable emotional response. Although that time is blurry, I remember many Ursulines I had barely met offering prayer and support; the heart of community was already reaching out to me.

Of course the transcontinental bike trip was off, and I even hesitated to go on into community. Although I worried for my mom, she was determined that I continue this journey in faith. As Dad's physical health improved and Mom seemed in control, my friend and I took a camping trip to Wyoming and the Grand Tetons—a jaunt that was to make up for the lost bike trip and help me "stock up on the out-of-doors" before I entered the convent.

By then, I was thirty-three years old and had searched for and followed my truths as I had found them. Through the journey into the Ursuline way I was, perhaps, seeking confirmation of these truths and my responses, a validation of my life choices—at least that's the way my mind worked. "As long as I see growth, the choice is true" was the measuring rod against which I assessed the validity of my Ursuline choice—a measuring rod that I would come to depend upon throughout my years of initial formation.

As a postulant with the Maple Mount Ursulines, I got to call myself "Sister"—just like that, with quotation marks. I lived in community at St. Pius X school and convent with three, sometimes four, other Ursulines. Each of us represented a different decade; from the thirties through the eighties, we spanned almost fifty years. I continued to teach in the public schools and completed my course work for my master of arts in education.

From the first meal at Pius X, which featured a large scoop of cottage cheese that I hate, to the last week's conversation when Sister Charles Asa who fretted that all our struggles must have made community seem awful, I grew. I ate the cottage cheese because I was ashamed to explain that I "couldn't stand its texture," and in that final week I had the courage to urge Sister Charles Asa to understand that the struggles simply proved that we believed community was worth working for. I was beginning to understand that the Ursulines did not simply allow community to emerge; they were committed to working for a true community whose unity of purpose could focus and magnify God's empowering love. I was ready for the novitiate—or so I thought.

For me, the novitiate was a once in a lifetime opportunity. Where else could a midlife professional drop out of the mainstream of life for a year of praying, reading, learning, and getting in touch with her God—all in a pastoral setting of hills, trees, and "fields, fallow and plowed," surrounded and supported by the example and prayer of Sisters who had given their lives in total commitment to God? But that was not to be a time of blissful reflection; it was to be a time of struggle and growth.

The dynamic of our diverse ages and experiences—I was thirty-five years old, the other novices were in their early twenties, and the directress of novices was thirty-six—created a great deal of tension in the midst of laughter, frivolity, and deep sharing. While the older Sisters provided inspiration, support, and friendship, their struggles challenged my understanding of faith within community—and their illnesses and infirmities made real my fears for my mom. The natural beauty of Mount Saint Joseph (the Mount) was not just idyllic and inspirational; it was an avenue for work and learning, and an opportunity for escape when I could not cope. Above all these considerations was the realization that I was being challenged to locate myself and my truths within the framework of a committed, covenantal community.

During that time, I was catapulted to unimagined heights and depths in my journey toward God. Two unbidden and recurring images penetrated and permeated my prayer—images that remain clear to me today. In one image, I walked alone, along wooded mountain paths, and emerged from the woods on a rocky crag where I gazed on a vista of mountains folded on mountains. Before me and below me, a lone figure walked with a staff. As I watched the figure disappear from sight in a cleft or tunnel, I knew I was meant to follow and that others would follow me.

The other image was of a tunnel through which I walked, but never alone. Sometimes my mysterious companions and I sought the light through the darkness, hints of its brightness only flickered ahead of us. Sometimes I carried light, bright and steady, and reached to give the light to those whose torches had flickered out. Always we were moving toward a light beyond all guessing, and always I knew that great joy and celebration surrounded the light. I reveled in the shared awareness of that joy.

After the first few months in the novitiate, I fell into a marathon of prayer. In ways I could never understand, I was sustained in hours upon hours of what surely approached contemplative prayer. This prayer would come in chapel, outside, alone, or with one or two others, and at times it would last the night. Always it was suffused with a wordless presence of God—sometimes great consolation, occasionally a nameless fear followed by that same gentle consolation. There were no words, just an overwhelming surrender to the enfolding, supporting, caring arms of God. In all my running to and from my God, I had never felt such peace.

Then, I awoke one morning and it was gone. I felt hollow. All my choices and all my truths seemed empty and false. There was no God. I counted up what was left in my Kentucky teachers' retirement fund, found an ad for a Mazda truck for $4,700, and plotted my course back to Dubois, Wyoming, where I could camp for three dollars a night until I could find a room. Sister Maureen, the novice directress, found me poring over the classified ads and, knowing me as she did, immediately sent me to Pennyroyal Girl Scout Camp. Perhaps she hoped that even in my darkness, I would find some solace in nature's silent witness to a God I could not touch; failing that, perhaps she hoped that a day at my cherished

Girl Scout camp might simply restore some balance to my soul.

Although it did not bring God back, that day in nature at least kept me from bolting. Many times, Dubois, Wyoming, would beckon me. Many times, I would sit in silence waiting for just a hint of God suggesting I go away. Many times, I would search the psalms for consolation. Many times, I would ask, "Am I going crazy?" and "Just what do these people believe anyway?" I was angry, hurt, lost, and afraid. What if all my choices had been wrong? I seemed to have no real alternative but to go forward with the Ursulines or to go back to Dubois.

The darkness remained, but slowly, more slowly than I could countenance, I found some peace with the empty darkness. I also found that the darkness was not empty. I began to realize that I was being called beyond my limited understanding of the holy and the sacred. Somehow in my searchings I had simply assumed that a personal relationship with God meant merely an individual relationship with God. I had also confused faith with a constant awareness of God's indwelling presence. I had to choose whether to remain desolate in my darkness or to remember the moments of light—both great and small—and journey on through the darkness in certain faith. Perhaps I was beginning to understand at last that faith is a gift given for the darkness.

My individual and limiting relationship with God was finally broken apart and, as long as I looked with eyes of faith, evidence of God's presence and passage was everywhere about me. God was revealed in the communities of people with whom I came in contact: the older and infirm Sisters with whom I worked at Mount Saint Joseph; the scouts—both young and old—with whom I volunteered; the students and the Sisters at Brescia College where I lived and taught; my Ursuline Sisters with whom I worked and played; my colleagues and fellow songsters at Purdue University where I completed my doctorate. As I have grown to see the God of love and hope within these diverse communities, I know I will never again be content with a private God. Even my solitude with God is enriched by an awareness of the greater community.

In my own person and among my Sisters, I have come to feel the supporting love of God as we rally to one another's aid—up to our elbows mixing tubs of potato salad for the annual picnic, coming in an unending line to cry with me when my dad died in 1989, and letting me weep and laugh as I journey with Mom in her long illness.

I have grown to recognize God as One who suffers and rejoices with us, enfleshed in our loving struggles as Maple Mount Ursulines. We have labored to learn to listen with respect to the fears and dreams of one another, and in so doing have dared to move as a community in new directions, expanding our understanding of witness and community. God forms and informs us, as we embrace healing ways of decision making, gentler relationships with the earth and others, and a hopeful stance for the future. As we experiment with greater reliance on communal discernment, challenge ourselves to use less more wisely, and embark on futuristic long-range plans, we continue to experience God's in-breaking Spirit in our lives and with one another.

I wonder now if Dad would agree that this Texas Baptist kiddo, this Maple Mount Ursuline, has "stuck to her guns." I know that I have searched for and followed God's truths as best I could, and that in the search, I have been blessed to find the Ursuline Sisters of Maple Mount. In their lives and in the lives of Saint Angela and all Ursulines, I have found myself within a community that searches as I do.

The one last truth of which I am now convinced is that God's empowering love cannot be kept within myself, within ourselves. My search, my task—our search, our task—is to share both the light and the journey with all we meet. This Texas Baptist will continue that journey in what I have come to regard as a marvelous company of women.

One Ordinary Life:
The Canadian Connection

ROSE-ANNE ENGEL, OSU

The whole creation waits in eager expectation for the children of God to be revealed.

—ROMANS 8:19

It was Sunday morning in my little village and all the farming community had gathered for church. They had come from three, ten, and twelve miles away, with their two- or four-wheel buggies drawn by giant, Clydesdale horses. Although many people still drove buggies with wheels made of wood, our Bennett buggy had real tires. Only a few people had cars. Horses shuffled in clusters while people stood around discussing whether it might rain. We were a motley crowd of German, French, English, and Irish—sons and daughters of the pioneers. It was 1939; Saskatchewan had been proclaimed a province of Canada twenty-five years ago.

I stood at the edge of the sun-bleached wooden sidewalk, silently watching. My hand-me-down dress just nibbled my white-ribbed stockings, while my silly hat—we all wore them—bent mischievously over my long curls. Mother had fashioned my curls just so, by putting up my thick, wet hair in even bunches of strands entwined in rags.

The Sisters came down the street two by two, hands enveloped in the endless folds of their black, surge, fingertip-length sleeves. They moved silently. They were what I believed to be holy: remote, unapproachable, the favoured of God. All the men respectfully removed their hats and curbed their conversations while the Sisters glided by, bowing solemnly to us, a slight smile creasing their lips as they passed silently into church. Although we all respected the Sisters, I was both terrified of them and attracted to them.

Earlier that morning I had been to the west edge of town, to the convent. Every Sunday morning, from the time I was knee-high to a grasshopper, I made my way to the convent door to take butter, cream, milk, eggs, or a chicken and occasionally a loaf of Mum's homemade bread to the Sisters. "Good morning, Sister. This is from Mum." "Thank you, my dear. God bless you. We will pray for you."

Something in Sister Agnes' black, laughing eyes always reached momentarily into that yet unnamed space within me and left its imprint for future reference. I never saw the inside of the convent and always felt a sense of relief as I skidaddled down the steps and ran back to visit with Grandpa, who lived in a one-room house in town. Thus unknown to me, my life journey with the Ursulines began. Other than summer school catechism, this was my only contact with the Sisters.

We referred to them as the Vibank Ursulines because their mother house was established in the village of Vibank in southern Saskatchewan in the early nineteen hundreds, one of three separate Ursuline congregations in Saskatchewan at the time: the Ursulines of Bruno, the Ursulines of Prelate, and the Ursulines of Vibank.

Our parish church in the town of Allan stood proudly amid the country pioneers. I remember the time I sang— solo—an old German hymn to Mary, *"Maria Zu Lieben"* ("I Love You O Mary"). I was only six years old at the time, and it seemed that my tiny voice echoed to the loft, through the bell tower, and across the prairies, leaving me feeling like I had done something holy. Every time I entered the church, I had that same sense, like I was entering into a world of holy wonder and grandeur—and somehow I was afraid of it. While the strange motions and unintelligible Latin sounds from the sanctuary billowed forth with the incense, I would wait for the moment when I could hug the marble altar rail to receive Communion. This, too, they said was holy, and mute row upon row of bowed heads and wind-ruddied faces acknowledged it. I was fascinated by the mystery and wondered in a kind of silent, childish awe.

Everyone in this farming community was dirt poor. The time was the end of the Depression and the beginning of World War II. Germany had just invaded Poland, September 1, 1939, and I had just started school: equally momentous landmarks in my history. Along with all the other farm children, I went to a one-room country school, where we filled the room to bulging with students from grade one to ten. The teacher always had the blackboard filled with work. I remember that I cried on one of my first days of school because I couldn't do all the work on the board. I was so amazed to discover that I had to do only the work marked, "Grade One." I had already learned to read at home from the cornflakes box. This came in handy to work ahead so I could spend all my free time reading from the wonderful store of books at the back of the room.

The country school became a haven of rest from farm work and a place to test our skills at the games of curling in the winter and gopher drowning in the spring and fall. In an effort to keep those pesky little rodents from destroying the odd blade of wheat that dared survive the drought, the municipality paid two cents for every gopher tail we could collect—but I don't know what our teacher did with all the tails we brought her.

School was also a place where we worded our experience of God in 123 memorized answers to questions. My total religious education was complete by the end of the second grade; thereafter it was a matter of fine tuning the recitation. Speed and accuracy was of the essence because our parish priest regularly came to the school to test us.

My cousin, Willie, sometimes had to kneel in the corner for not being in church on Sunday. Willie, a little older than I and the oldest in his family, occasionally had to stay home from church on Sunday to care for the farm animals, especially in winter. I felt sorry for him one time and lied, saying that I, too, was not in church that Sunday, just to keep Willie company in his misery in the corner.

Like so many other farming families on the Canadian prairies, we suffered one crop failure after the other during the Depression. The war not only meant continued deprivation and rationing of food stuffs, but it threatened the loss of essential farm labour which had been provided by the young men who were being conscripted to serve in the armed forces. My oldest brother, Roy, failed the medical test for conscription, however, because of a ruptured appendix, so our family was spared. This did not improve the drought in our fields and the rationing in our larders, though he had given up finishing his education to run the farm.

To my two oldest sisters, Bernie and Eleanor, fell the lot of working indoors and outdoors, as they tried to juggle finishing high school with the backbreaking labour required for the survival of the farm. As teenagers, they were often bone weary, and today, Bernie often says, "I was born tired."

My sister, Addie, was born seven-and-a-half years after I. Of all the children in the world, Addie seemed to me to be the greatest child that ever graced the face of the earth. As a little sister, she was not only intelligent and adorable, she was the only one who could make our father relax his predilection that faith, discipline, hard work, and knowledge were what it took to make us into great human beings. Dad would carry

Addie down the country road, sing to her, and generally lavish an affection on her that none of us had never seen before. This did not make Addie's growing years much easier, for, as each of the older children left home, she and I had to assume the work left behind. My three sisters have always edified me with their positive and humorous outlook on past times, and today I treasure the fact that we are great friends as well as sisters.

Times were difficult in the forties. My father was a proud man and as a provider, he agonized until the last waterless blade of wheat died and our scarecrow cows presented shrivelled, milkless udders. Only then would he succumb to the Relief Program, a kind of food assistance program provided by our government, consisting of barrels of little green, wormy apples or crates of smoked herring. We survived because we had flour made from our own stored wheat which Mum could transform, by adding water and a bit of the ration of salt, into countless varieties of noodles.

As for Mum, her day never ended. Long after we were in bed for the night, and I would need to go to the outhouse, I would see her sitting in the "front room" (our living room), praying the rosary. No doubt her prayers were for better times ahead. Her schooling had come to an abrupt end after Grade Eight so she could work to help her family survive hard times. As the saying goes, she was the heart of the family.

As people of simple faith, my parents trusted that God would see us through the Depression. They never failed to believe that things would be better tomorrow. Theirs was not a foreign God who led the people out of the motherland; rather providence justified their hope. We had come to know our place. God was Someone to whom we bent our knee and before whom we crossed ourselves to signal our entrance into the holy, there to accept and be satisfied. For us children, respect for the mystery that was God flowed out into our attitudes toward adults as well. *"Gelobtzei Jesus Christus"* ("Praise be Jesus Christ") we used to say as we passed a grownup, and the answer was always, *"In alle Evigkeit kind"* ("Forever and ever, Child").

Not that we spoke of God and holy things; rather, God and the holy spoke to us. How we knew that fact remains a mystery, but we knew it. Faith simply described everything without words. It was the reason the Germans came to the prairie region of Canada in the first place. This western Canadian land promised freedom from the Bolsheviks and later from the Nazis. Its virgin soil promised growth and life for body and soul. No one could break the faith that had built the character of those who broke free from the barbed wire fences and the concentration camps. Hope bent persevering backs to the plow, urging the six horses down the mile-long furrows being readied for the seed that would bring a rich harvest.

I listened silently to the stories told around our dining table by friends from the neighbouring farms about the tears of separation from parents, cousins, brothers, and sisters who were lost in the games of war played by men. I was in the process of inheriting something much too big to understand.

Both my parents were children of immigrants. Along with my three sisters and two brothers, I grew up the fifth in the family, in an environment of discipline and hard work. Knowing what was expected of us was a given; we didn't need to be told or taught how to do things. It was assumed. This environment prepared me for my life as an Ursuline Sister of Prelate.

It was my fifteenth year and I had decided to join my friend, who was seventeen, and become a Sister of Saint Martha, in Antigonish, in the Maritimes. It was not that the Ursulines of Vibank would not have satisfied my desire to be a Sister.

It's that at fifteen, I was more easily influenced by my friend's power of persuasion.

A friend of the family intervened, however, when he wrote me a letter from Prelate in southern Saskatchewan, where he was stationed as the parish priest. He simply asked when I would be coming to the Ursuline convent, at Prelate. After all, they had a good boarding school and I was old enough to be a Sister. My plans changed.

About this time, my brother, Norbert, celebrated the Perpetual Profession of Vows with the Oblates of Mary Immaculate. Norbert was somewhat of a genius; he had finished high school at fifteen and had entered the seminary immediately after that. I didn't know him very well because he left home when he was twelve; I was only seven. Nevertheless, I cried all day. Perhaps it had something to do with the fact that I was to leave home two days later myself—or perhaps it had to do with the grandeur of the moment, my brother's vows, and my decision to become a Sister. I was overwhelmed.

On November 3, 1948, in the midst of a raging blizzard, I left by train from a neighbouring town to go to the Prelate Ursuline convent boarding school. It was a long, roundabout trip, my first alone. When the train stopped for three hours at Swift Current, a city ninety miles from Prelate, I ate at a nearby restaurant and went to an Ozzie and Harriet movie in the local cinema.

Later that evening I was welcomed warmly to Saint Angela's convent. Because the other boarders had already settled in, I was a novelty for a while. Being a "convent girl" was a lot easier than harnessing horses much too big for a small girl, making hay, and stooking. It was easy to get up at six-fifteen. At home I often had four cows milked, the calves and other animals fed, and the cream separated from the milk and cooling in the icehouse by that time. Being able to read and study was heaven.

Maggie, Betty, and I formed a triad of friends, and being in Grade Ten at the convent school became a never-ending party. With little else to do but learn, we excelled in things like crawling down the fire escape in the evening to see if we could manage to do it without getting caught. Scaling the fire escape also allowed us to take off for downtown or to sneak off to the kitchen for a late-night snack.

Gradually, we grew out of our childish pranks and on January 6, 1949, just three months after I had come to Prelate, I entered as a postulant of the Ursuline Sisters—a turning point that did more than meet my burning desire to become a Sister. I had grown out of the few meagre clothes I had brought with me. Putting on the black, slightly below-the-knee length, surge dress of the postulants brought out a whole new me. I looked and felt at least eighteen. I also wore the solemn demeanour of a full-fledged nun with a mission. I'd work on holiness later.

The Ursulines of Prelate had a reputation throughout Saskatchewan for their emphasis on the fine arts as well as excellence in teaching. People came from miles to see the three-act plays that included actors who were boarders, local townsfolk, farmers, and even Sisters. As daughters of German immigrant parents living in rural Saskatchewan, the Sisters remained close to the ordinary people. Stressing participation in the arts was only one example of this and, in fact, remains an important aspect of our identity today. Our academy is the only Catholic girls' boarding school operating in western Canada today.

At the invitation of Father Riedinger, O.M.I., the "Prelate Sisters," as we are often called, were founded in 1919, by Mother Clementia Grafeldar, who had emigrated from Koln, Germany. The Sisters had the same courageous, efficient, and persevering character that brought our families through the Depression and World War II. Here, too, the holy manifested itself in the songs that swelled the hand-painted chapel walls and echoed in every Hail Mary that flowed from our lips as we washed the pots and pans. As each of my newfound Sisters took on a personality and character of her own, my impression of the Sisters in Allan in my growing-up years slowly receded. I was at home.

Experience leaves its mark. Such was the experience of the convent root cellar, a garden vegetable storage room dug deep beneath the earth, about a stones-throw away from the convent—a handy space in the days before refrigerators were affordable; there I spent a part of my novitiate. That huge cavern in the ground held all the fresh food for the winter for the Sisters. There, we novices spent part of our work time sorting the good vegetables from the spoiled, ripping the new shoots off the potatoes, and separating the wilty from the not-so wilty. It was there, to my amazement, that I discovered the prayer of work. No words were uttered other than the rosary and litany, keeping track of the Hail Marys by prefacing each one with the words, "the first choir of angels," "the second choir of angels," and so forth. It was efficient; we never messed up our sorting or our counting. More than that, there was time to learn to focus, to become single-minded, to keep our ideas and thoughts on the Lord, or at least to ourselves. We never lost our sense of humour, however; Betty made certain of that. Occasionally a limp beet or a dried up carrot was given a toss, narrowly missing the starched collars and bandeaux of the religious habit of the more serious among us. In the silent presence of the Lord, while we discerned the fate of the cabbages and corn, I took another step in my understanding of God.

By the time I left the novitiate, I was Ursuline. We learned the history of the Ursulines of Prelate and assimilated the character, spirit, and life of that "beacon light on the great prairie." In two years we learned the stories, the experiences, and the struggles of the missions (our houses on the prairies) as if we had been there and experienced them ourselves.

Sister Rose, our novice directress, was a marvellous story-teller. She could laugh and cry with equal vigour as she re-counted the congregation's struggles during the twenties, thir-ties, and forties: the fires, the joys, the pain, and the ever-present, holy God who directed, formed, and blessed the Ursuline community. We heard of the days when the Anderson government forced the Sisters out of their habits so that they could continue teaching in the public schools, and about the days when the Sisters had nothing to eat for a week other than the few rations of coffee, flour, salt, and but-ter that they received during their weekend visit to the mother house. We heard how the Sisters taught in one-room country schools and how goading a taciturn horse that carried them in a buggy during spring and fall, and in an open cutter (a sort of horse-drawn sled) in winter, got them where they needed to go. We heard of the indignities heaped upon the Sisters by a few who disfavoured their teaching in public schools, and we marvelled at their courage, perseverance, com-mitment to education, and faith. I became proud of my newly acquired heritage. My religious formation as a Sister had be-gun. I fell in love with the Sisters and became missionary-minded. I couldn't wait to get out there to join the "mission Sisters."

In our congregation there were two basic roles: teaching or managing the household. So along with the unintelligible meanderings of Garagoue Lagrange, Rodrigue, and the *Tirochineum Religiosum*, we learned the Ursuline method of education during our three-year preparation for perpetual profession. Whereas the two-year novitiate immersed us in the Ursuline way of life with its emphasis on loyalty, respect, and the presence of God, the three-year time of temporary profession was to mold our hearts and widen our theological horizons. The study of the vows and the life and writings of Saint Angela completed our training. Secretly, and with a small flashlight that I kept stored under the sheets of my bed, I also read other such worthwhile works, such as Zane Gray's great western novels and the *Book of Knowledge*. I felt I was getting a well-rounded formation in religious life. My passage to perpetual profession surely was assured!

After three years, however, it seemed like I knew less and less about praying and more and more about things to do or not do to make myself holy. My earliest notion of the holy through my experiences on the farm was being severely tested. I knew the kid could be taken out of the farm, but I wasn't about to allow the farm to be taken out of the kid. Trying to acquire perfection gave me the most trouble. Acquiring perfection—to make ourselves more pleasing to God—through odd practices and self-denial stood in stark contrast to the already all-present God playing before me in the Aurora Borealis and waving in the free flowing golden grain of the mile-long wheat field just outside the back door of the convent. Becoming perfect didn't make that more evident. The God of my childhood simply did not need to be enticed with odd practices and fervent invocations; God was already so much there.

At seventeen, the confidence and sense of responsibility that came at an early age with caring for livestock and handling heavy machinery on the farm gave way to uncertainty and fear that comes of not wanting to make a mistake. Using common sense in making decisions on the farm gave way to getting permission to do the most trivial tasks. The whole idea, of course—being corrected for every wayward action—

was to teach me to be perfect, and thus qualify me for perpetual vows. But wasn't I already the handiwork of God? It was with a huge sense of relief that I received the news that I was to pack immediately and go teach in a rural school to replace a Sister who had become ill.

My first experience outside the mother house! I was seventeen years old and, in addition to the studies of a temporary professed Sister, I was completing Grade Eleven, which had been interrupted for my novitiate. This stunning turn of events in my life, far from discouraging me, became a way to recapture my initial enthusiasm. I was finally going to be one of the Sisters in "the missions," our term for our small convents scattered across the prairies in rural Saskatchewan. My suitcase, containing three habits and my Grade Eleven textbooks, was packed by ten-thirty—half an hour after I was informed of the assignment. I called this event an intervention by God.

No one questioned that I had not yet been to teachers' college. There was a shortage of teachers in Saskatchewan in the early fifties, so the government accepted "temporary Sitters." These were persons like myself who had not been trained as teachers but who presided over a classroom of students until the regular teacher could return. Because Sister Bernarda's recuperation ended up being long term, I taught every subject—except music and art—to a class of forty-five students in Grades Four and Five, for the full term. In the evenings I corrected and prepared assignments for my students and studied my own Grade Eleven courses. Except for chemistry and mathematics, my own studies were a snap. I am probably the only person who passed chemistry without ever doing an experiment. Ron, a Grade Eleven student in the school where I was teaching, occasionally helped me with math. I never admitted that he was nearly my own age. He was a tough, strong youth, and goodness flowed from his personality. Whenever

I supervised the Grade Eleven and Twelve class, while Sister Mercedes taught music and art in my class, Ron stood at the back of the class and simply stated to the rest of the students, "Anyone move and you're dead." He saved my life.

Life in our mission homes was a freeing experience. That didn't mean I loved the mother house less; it was just that the small convent was more like a home, and teaching gave us the contact with peoples' lives—something I had missed for three years. Our evening recreations together were filled with the details of our day and the latest political scam. It provided a refreshing break from Lagrange and Rodrigue. It was real living, and I was happy.

In fact, during this time I became acquainted with Saint Teresa of Avila. Her *Way of Perfection* and *The Interior Castle* caught my imagination. I put away the *Tirochineum* and read, instead, the wild tales of her life, reforms, and prayer—and discovered someone whose God was not removed and distant; God was Someone real to her. I wasn't so caught up in her mystical experience as I was transfixed by her zeal and undaunted courage.

In my enthusiasm and fervour for copying Teresa's character, I failed to take notice of whether I was teaching anything of consequence to the eager nine- and ten-year-olds in front of me. Somehow I muddled through, knowing that if I erred I would be told.

The following year, having successfully passed my Grade Eleven departmental exams, I was asked to teach in yet another rural school. Armed again with my own textbooks—for Grade Twelve—I taught school during the day and studied at night. I was getting good at that.

I suppose I was lucky that I was not canonically old enough to celebrate my perpetual profession as an Ursuline Sister of

Prelate at the end of my three-year preparation for vows. I had that extra year to "catch up," as it were, with the others.

When finally I did get to teachers' college, in the extra year before perpetual profession, I have to confess that I genuinely hated every minute of it. The classes appeared to have little to do with my own experiences in the classroom. I never studied. Instead, I read the Greek and Roman philosophers and other entirely irrelevant authors. I had the opportunity to read such books as *Cry the Beloved Country* and to attempt my skills at deciphering the inchoate blathering of William Faulkner, whom I later learned to enjoy.

I wasn't the youngest in class anymore, for I was now twenty years old. After one year I graduated with a Standard A Certificate, and was officially a teacher. When I was assigned to teach forty-one students in Grades One, Two, and Three in a public school in Saskatchewan, I felt just a twinge of regret for not taking my Primary Methods Class a bit more seriously.

Since it was a public school, I couldn't wear any religious symbol such as the rosary, and I couldn't display a cross or any holy pictures in my classroom unless they were school-approved paintings of certain artists. So, Leonardo da Vinci's *Last Supper* hung on the walls of every classroom occupied by the Sisters—right next to the portrait of the Queen. At three-thirty every day when school was dismissed, the Protestant children went home while the Catholic children remained for catechism classes. Only then were all the cupboard doors opened to display the holy pictures and charts of the Catholic faith that we had carefully concealed. The display transformed the atmosphere of the classroom and made teaching catechism a half hour of joy.

I loved teaching. It gave me the opportunity I'd been waiting for: I was, at last, the "missionary." It wasn't exactly the jungles of Africa, but it would do.

During that time, and in the ensuing years of teaching the primary grades in the city of Saskatoon, my prayer life began to suffer. The days slipped by in feverish activity, and there never seemed to be enough hours in the day to prepare and correct assignments—and pray. I was not a morning person, so I slept through most of the six o'clock common meditation time. Only my love for singing kept me awake during Mass at six-forty-five. I became an expert in taking two-minute naps in my bed between Mass and breakfast: a trick that helped me awaken for the onslaught of the day. Whatever part of my self that hadn't come alive by nine was shocked into reality by the forty Grade One students who met me at the classroom door for the next eight hours.

In conversation with a Sister one day, I came to understand that approaching God in prayer did not necessarily mean saying a lot of words. In fact, prayer often meant no words at all. I asked Sister what she did when she sat in our little chapel at night. Her answer startled me: "I sit and give God a chance to say whatever is on God's mind, and then I have my say. I place myself in the presence of God, clear my brain, and wait for God to have a say. If God doesn't have anything to say, fine. I have my say and go to bed."

Great, but clearing my brain was no easy task; it aped a television screen with its ceaseless and fragmented commentary on useless bits of information stored there. I even prepared some of my best lesson plans during prayer—when I wasn't sleeping.

"All the words and the colloquies," Sister continued, "are chaff to be blown from the kernel—the Word remains. Nothing must stand between you and God. Just give your distractions to God." Now that was a novel thought; that sounded like freedom to me, and the choices I might make would be the fruit of that freedom.

Although the frugal fifties were gradually replaced by the promising early sixties in Saskatchewan, the Sisters' teaching salaries remained poor. They didn't cover the cost of building our own houses, paying property taxes, buying cars, and finishing our degrees in education. A more economical alternative to long-term leaves of absence to study for our degrees was to attend night classes and summer sessions.

Times improved in the late sixties, and in 1968 I went to Ottawa University for a two-year program, to complete a bachelor of arts degree in religious studies. I was just in time to greet the "death-of-God" theologians. This new theology was significant for me because through my studies in Ottawa I realized how much the God of my childhood, a distant and unapproachable God, had truly been totally present in all things. During my childhood years, I had approached God in reverential fear; during my early years as a religious, that same God had become mysteriously tangled in a web of unusual ascetical practices and self-denials that left my prayer a repetition of pious invocations through which I might gain indulgences and merit heaven—or at least a lesser purgatory. Through my experience at the University, I found a fresh dimension of God as Someone who speaks in the very core of my being.

Somehow, despite myself and all my railings against foreign practices and peculiar spiritual exercises, I must have been in touch with this faithful God. The "death-of-God" theorists challenged me to lay to rest the concept of God as remote and unapproachable and to begin to see that a spiritual life meant a personal relationship with God. As far as I was concerned at the time, I did not have that kind of comfort and intimacy with God. I was faithful to prayer and to the community practices; I was even fervent. But nothing had touched my soul. In those years at Ottawa my original sense of wonder and awe returned to become transformed into a sense of trust in and with God—and in and with others.

Eucharist, for example, took on new meaning for me: Communion with God and communion with others. It became a time to discover friendship as opposed to avoiding "particular friendships," as we had been trained. I discovered that the beauty in friendship is no less a sign of God's presence than the solitary attentiveness encountered in the stillness of a night chapel or the crackling, colorful playfulness of the Aurora Borealis of my youth.

My growth did not happen in isolation; it was supported and encouraged by the persevering and faithful growth of the community. This steady growth and development, however, was accompanied by a sense of restlessness, a movement for change in our way of life, encouraged by the Vatican Council. Our congregation had come through four difficult and trying decades: we were expanding our mission houses; spiritual growth was fostered through education in theology and Scripture; we found a voice to proclaim our hopes to lead a new life in keeping with the times; vocations to our congregation were flourishing.

Many of us no longer viewed the discipline of an earlier monastic lifestyle, reinforced in the forties and early fifties, as the only way to live out our consecrated life of love and service. In fact, some saw it as an oppressive structure to apostolic ministry. Personally, I saw it as a meddlesome affront to my own fledgling awakening to a sense of real womanhood.

These views, however, were hardly welcomed universally throughout the congregation. We could not have predicted how deeply the more conservative views would come into conflict with the newfound hope for a more independent and freer lifestyle. Division in the community resulted. The mutual suffering shared by many strengthened my resolve to support the effort to breathe the "fresh air" promised by the Second Vatican Council. I was delighted and edified by our leadership. They, among others in the community, encouraged us to open the doors of discussion that were never to close again.

For a while, however, I straddled Mars and Venus. Sometimes I didn't know whose side I was on; I didn't even know what the sides were. All I knew was that something momentous was about to happen—and it did. I was excited at the prospects for change toward a new emphasis on the apostolic life of the community.

Renewal came to be the word on everyone's lips. Who are we? Are these the right questions? What are the questions? We went on and on. It was during this time that late-night refreshment breaks were invented. For me, it was a time to probe, query, and trust my best friends in the community with ideas, hopes, and dreams. I was certain that together we could formulate a new way of life that would be filled with the very spirit Jesus promised: "I came that [you] may have life, and have it abundantly" (John 10:10). To be good educators was not enough. We were more. We were also women, road-weary women stilted by lives that had been compelled to root in the narrow ruts of the patriarchal system, keeping us obedient and loyal at any cost. I was encouraged to see that we were women on the move, and heaven only knows where that would lead us. Happily, for me, it took us to a rediscovery of Saint Angela who, perhaps more than ever before, spoke to our time: "For your part, lead a new life."

Angela never spoke of vows but of total giving. She did not speak of community but of a sense of companionship, of "communion." Only much later did her vision of "communion" become narrowed to mean an apostolic community. I wondered, as did most of us during that time, about what she meant by "new life." The needs in the Church and society were not new. Rather, the "new life" needed to be manifested in new ways through new ministries other than teaching. It implied incorporating new prayer forms that would accommodate a more flexible lifestyle and a people of God with whom we could share our lives and our prayer. These strands of thought hounded my aching brains for days on end.

As a community, we argued, discussed, and wrote reams of proof for our highly innovative resolutions. "The religious dress will be simple and modest." "The cross and the ring will be the symbol of her religious dress." "Ministry will dictate where an Ursuline of Prelate lives." Area communities, associates, ongoing formation: we reworded and rewrote, and finally had our revised Constitutions, a process that energized and enriched me.

Months of preparation culminated in a six-week Ursuline summer convention, after which I returned to ministry with a new experimental Constitution—"The Ursuline Way of Life"—and a new affection for those who participated in the process. It had been like a yearlong getting-reacquainted party with one another and with our own roots. The impact was felt only much later.

The danger with renewal and change, of course, is that we might simply trade one cage for another. Angela's simple motto, "Be ready to go wherever you are needed and do whatever God wants," encouraged us to diversify, but it also triggered a certain self-serving me-ism for a few. I was very troubled by this and harboured a growing concern to understand the difference between a healthy self-identity and a selfish preoccupation with individualism. I could see clearly that we were stronger for taking responsibility for our own spiritual lives and in making collaborative decisions regarding ministry. The path into an unknown and uncertain future in religious life with a transition from a monastic lifestyle to a lifestyle of greater freedom where all the rules of the game had changed, however, de-

manded a collaborative spirit and a generosity that could not
be endangered by me-ism.

As the sixties gave way to the early seventies, we had to
redefine both the meaning of religious life and the meaning
of trust. I wanted to see that trust in God's Spirit, trust in the
sincerity and the collective common sense and intelligence of
one another, and trust in the promises of Saint Angela worked
together to become the framework for our renewed lives. I
came to understand that the challenge lay somewhere in the
seemingly contradictory statement that in order to move forward, we had to go back. Trust became a key word.

Saint Angela took centre stage; she became my mentor.
We had come home. Whereas Angela didn't speak of communal life, she encouraged us to build unity and harmony
of purpose. Whereas she didn't speak of any particular apostolic life, she lived committed to the Lord—a pilgrim—
ready to go wherever God wanted. The sacred with which I
had become acquainted in early childhood lived on in Angela and in her daughters, the Ursulines. We were ready to
do what she encouraged. "If, with the needs of the times,
change is necessary, do it with prudence and courage," she said.
We were building a new community. We were shaping our
own future according to the spirit and charism of Angela.

It was both exciting and awesome for me. We had done
something of extreme importance and consequence. For the
most part we rose to the challenge. In time we realized the
magnitude of the effect of some of our changes. The same
vision which gave inspiration to most encouraged others to
leave the congregation to lead lives committed to the Church
in other ways.

As I rejoiced in our newfound hope, I wept for our losses.
Lifelong friends chose another path in their journey to God.
Symbolic of this moment in our history was the occasion of
my silver jubilee in 1976. While I rejoiced in God's faithful-

ness in my life I also shed tears that I was the only one left in my group to celebrate my silver jubilee. They remembered me, however, with a suitably engraved silver tray and their unfailing love.

During the time of renewal, I had been appointed the Religion Consultant of the Catholic Schools in the city of Saskatoon, a city whose population was growing rapidly due to the newfound wealth of bumper crops and the discovery of oil. My sheltered life as an elementary teacher in Saskatoon and Swift Current came to an end. With encouragement from the community, I was given a leave of absence from the Catholic school board in 1978 to study for a master's degree in religious studies at Gonzaga University in Spokane, Washington. I fell in love with reading and studying the New Testament.

Ultimately my master's thesis personified for me the path to God my life was taking: *Communion Between Jesus and God and Communion Between Jesus and the Disciple.* A somewhat dry exegesis of some of the relevant passages in John's Gospel, it nevertheless became for me a time to come to understand more clearly God's action in my life as a transforming action of grace. Fidelity to God's abiding presence became rather the abiding fidelity of God in my life and in the life of the Church.

In 1983, after thirty-four years of religious life, I was elected the coordinator of our General Convention and subsequently was elected general superior of our congregation for a four-year term. This was followed by reelection in 1987. I remained in leadership until 1991. At this time in my life, more than at any other, I learned in a new way the meaning of community support, sisterly friendship, family love, and trust in God's Providence.

The wrenching experience of my mother's death due to a sudden heart attack happened early in my term in leadership, while she was waiting at the bus depot to come visit me on Halloween Day in October 1983. This experience tested me as nothing else ever had. In the ten years before that day we had become friends. This may appear strange at first glance, but my early departure at age fifteen and the early rules of the congregation which restricted our visits home had not given me an opportunity to get to know her very well. We now had formed a relationship of trust and were able to tell each other about the hopes and fears that accompanied our daily life. We prayed, sang, shopped, told stories, ate out, and laughed together. Living only forty miles from Saskatoon, my mother had become a sort of buddy to a number of Sisters through her frequent visits to the convent. Part of my soul died with her that day and the meaning of real compassion was born in me by the outpouring of care and concern shown by all the Sisters, especially those with whom I lived.

In addition to the ongoing formation and spiritual development of each Sister, the issues of justice, equality rights, and abuse of women and others became central themes in my first term in leadership.

Doug, ex-con and ex-"Big Mamma" of a notorious gang in Eastern Canada, now "born again," showed up in my office. The tattoos on both arms gave me a "watch your back" feeling. But his blue eyes were gentle. He had lost a leg when someone from his past tried to even a score by shooting him as he was riding home on his Harley. Part of Doug's brain was damaged from prolonged use of heroin. He could no longer read and write. That didn't deter Doug who was on a mission. He wanted to set up a place and a program for the rehabilitation of drug addicts and prostitutes. Someone had told him to go to the Ursuline Generalate in Saskatoon. They would help. Along with the generosity of the Oblates, a house was soon functioning and by word of mouth the women began to show up on the doorstep. The "Be ye perfect" of Matthew's Gospel became Luke's "Be ye compassionate" for me.

It is no longer an exception to see Sisters minister to those who are vulnerable and defenceless. AIDS patients, single moms, battered women, the homeless, are no longer just subjects for table conversation but are now objects of our concerned love in all our ministries.

I have tried to articulate some aspects of my life which most significantly speak of the sense of God in my life. There are many more. Threshing machines have long given way to combines and the old Underwood typewriters have given way to computers. Today classroom and cloister reside where there is still one person who has not received the fullness she has inherited equally. The sense of God remains. God is the holy and the holy is to be found in everything and everyone. God is approachable and lives in the heart of each of us. Perhaps my most important task today is to give witness to my growing sense of outrage and that of the community, at the snail's pace effort made by those who control power, in creating initiatives which could lead to a more just environment especially as it relates to women. The war games continue in board rooms and in reality while the gulf of dissent grows wider.

As part of the Church that speaks clearly on the social ills of our time, it is clear that I have to do whatever I can to stand with the victims of our sinful capitalist society. And more often than not the victims are women and the elderly. The Scriptures and the social documents of the Church provide the foundation for us to create a web of interconnectedness that goes beyond the gender dimension and which can create a unity, harmony, and dignity for all.

It's a long and weary struggle for me and perhaps the only way to make a difference is to make a stand. The difference at the global level is begun at the individual level. This stand has led me to law school. Through the law, I hope to say that at least here in this tiny spot on the prairies in Canada and at this time in my life:

> *I am with you in your struggle.*
> *Maybe I can even make a difference*
> *to re-envision and reshape*
> *this tiny segment of the world*
> *where we still hear the tired drama that,*
> *"Men will glory and women must weep."*
> —NELLIE McLUNG

I will be there with you, until we have eliminated the social conditioning expressed by Lisa Freedman in the startling line "that woman's place in society has too often been recorded on the receiving end of a fist" (Lisa Freedman). I look with hope at the men and women who stand together everywhere today in a common search for ways to "wipe every tear from their eyes" and to build a world where there will be "no more death or mourning, crying out or pain, for the former world has passed away" (Revelations 21:4).

So Fill Your Horizon

DIANNE BAUMUNK, OSU

I know the plans I have in mind for you—
it is Yahweh who speaks—plans for peace, not disaster,
reserving a future full of hope for you.
When you seek me, you will find me.
When you seek me with all your heart, I will let you find me.
*—*JEREMIAH 29:11,13

My life has been an exploration through a vast land-scape of people and experiences, bringing me home to my-self. Each rock and tree and heart has played a part. As I tell my story, I mingle significant moments and insights of past and present, spiraling deeper and deeper into the reality of who I have been called to be as a companion of Angela Merici.

As a first-grader I experienced my first funeral, that of our third-grade teacher, Sister Mary George, whom every-one loved. Coming home from the funeral, I shared with my mother the sadness I felt over Sister Mary George being gone, and I announced that I would grow up and take her place. No one was surprised that I would think of shouldering that re-sponsibility so naturally, and I never doubted that I would do just that. At the young age of six, I was already the caretaker of the family, feeding and caring for my mother who was confined to bed during a difficult pregnancy. No matter that

I could make only tomato sandwiches and marmalade on toast; I took my responsibility seriously.

Unwavering in my responsibilities, I was also recklessly committed to whatever I believed in. Through my youth in the sixties, for example, my parents lived in fear and trepidation that I would take radical action on my convictions, imagining that I would marry the first black man I met to prove that interracial marriage could work. After I entered the convent, my mother continued to worry about my recklessness toward commitment. She was afraid that I would never leave the convent even if I were terribly unhappy, because I would stubbornly stick to my commitment, right or wrong. I can't say that those fears were wholly ungrounded.

At the age of eight, I fell in love with Saint Francis of Assisi, who was so radical that he tore off his clothes in the crowded village square and gave himself totally to God. Francis was a crazy man, talking to birds and trusting a ravaging wolf. I loved him wildly and hoped to be as crazy myself.

In the crazy spirit of Saint Francis, I entered the Ursuline novitiate. Preparing for final vows in 1972, I gave my local superior my letter to Rome requesting acceptance for final profession. Handing it back with a worried look, she asked if I really intended to tell Mother General that a person would have to be crazy to stay with this way of life and that since I was that crazy, of course, she should accept me. My response? Yes, I did intend to say all that—and I did—and having said it, I was still accepted. Twenty-five years later, my thirty-day retreat began with a reading from Saint Paul asking, "Are you out of your mind?" The answer was still "yes"!

Religious life is far from easy for a crazy idealistic dreamer. The journey of this dreamer, though packed with adventurous tales and laughter, is spotted with tears, disillusionment, and lessons well worth the learning.

Born in 1946 the oldest of five and the first grandchild on both sides of the family, I grew up taking for granted the responsibility and high expectations heaped upon me as the oldest child. I sometimes wonder if I had a childhood at all; it seems I was always working. My parents believed we should grow up having chores and responsibilities.

Although Dad was a carpenter/contractor, we usually lived on small farms in rural California. We raised our own meat and produce, and sometimes even realized a cash crop. One year Mom and I raised twenty acres of black-eyed peas to earn extra money for the luxury of a dishwasher.

At age ten or twelve I was too young to pack crates of sweet corn tightly enough for market, but I drove the tractor for the picking crew. The pumphouse was lined with the fruits of our labor and the artistry of our canning: beans, peaches, applesauce, and jellies. Some of my fondest childhood memories revolve around stirring those cooking kettles of fruit, picking berries in the quiet of morning, and churning the cream into butter. Those were my favorite chores because they had a reflective rhythm to them and were special times for me and Mom to be together and talk.

As I grew up, shouldering more and more responsibility and achieving higher and higher goals, the message I remember hearing was not one of praise for my abilities but one of criticism for my inadequacies and incompetence—so that I wouldn't get a big head. The focus was not on the A's on the report card, but on that one B+; obviously, I was not quite measuring up. When I decided to become a nun, my father said that the Sisters would probably send me straight home as soon as they discovered how messy I was.

At an early age, I began to sense that something was not right in my family, but I had no idea what the problem was. I noticed certain family patterns, like feelings not being expressed, affection not being shown, silence being the norm in handling conflict. No one talked about drinking, much less alcoholism. Even now I don't know if my three brothers would admit that Dad is an alcoholic or that we have all been affected. Although my father was a hard worker and good provider, and we appeared to be a model Catholic family, something was missing emotionally.

Dad would come home from work, milk the cow—which Mom made us promise never to admit we knew how to do—eat dinner, and then fall asleep in front of the TV many beers later. It seemed an empty life to me. I could not understand why my father did not seem to "be there" for us—and I could not imagine why my mother stayed in a relationship that offered her so little.

I do remember wonderful times when Dad and I would swim out beyond the ocean breakers and backfloat companionably. I remember a few shopping sprees with Dad when I was a teenager: the sleeping bag we purchased that I still have, and the time we went to pick up my study desk and came home with my brand-new car (although I wasn't even old enough to drive). Dad bought me things, but we didn't talk—and that just wasn't enough for me.

I was sure of one thing: I didn't want to end up with a hollow life. I believed relationships were important, and I wanted nothing more than to live in a religious community and fill my life with people. Although my own family experience didn't bear it out, I grew up with the firm belief that if I worked hard enough, I could make any relationship work. No matter what the problem, I could put up with anything to prove I really cared, and I believed that kind of sacrificial love could and would change people.

Out of my own deep-seated fears of abandonment grew my dominant strength: a compassion that drives me to be all the more committed to being there for others. Sometimes this starts as an attempt to change someone and prove myself, but along the way, real love develops.

When I was in college in Washington, D.C., as a junior professed, for example, I did volunteer work at Saint Elizabeth's, a mental hospital. Part of a tutoring team that gave patients (considered "hopeless cases") interaction with "normal" people, I was drawn to one particular woman. Everyone kept their distance from Geraldine, as she had a sharp tongue and could be abusive, physically as well as verbally. I was determined, though, to break through her wall. She wanted to learn to read again, so that's where we started with our rocky relationship.

Geraldine had been sold as a prostitute by her own mother. When Geraldine contracted syphilis, her mother did not get her treatment until the disease had progressed so far that a large portion of Geraldine's brain had been eaten away. The doctors thought Geraldine would never walk again, but by sheer determination, she did. The paralysis also left her speech impaired. Some sounds were impossible for Geraldine to make, and what she could articulate often took careful deciphering. Few people had the patience to untangle Geraldine's comments, which left her communicating to no avail most of the time. In her frustration, Geraldine could be fierce and unpredictable.

Geraldine was accustomed to being "used," and anger was her dominant disposition. While she suspected everyone else of being out to use or abuse her, she could not accept the fact that her own mother had used and abused her tragically. As a result, she had constructed a lovely fantasy around her mother—and took her anger out on everyone else.

There were times when I would go home elated that I had seen a tiny crack in Geraldine's wall, maybe because I had glimpsed the promise of a smile around her eyes. There were other times when I despaired. But no matter how bad

Geraldine behaved or how frightened I was of her anger, I never gave up on her—and patience and persistence won out in the end. We eventually developed a caring, respectful relationship.

I knew what Geraldine would feel when I had to tell her that I would soon graduate from college and return to California; I know how it is to feel abandoned. Fortunately, we've kept in touch over the years, and I have never forgotten the lesson in love that she taught me. I did not change Geraldine; she changed her own behavior in response to an environment of love that asked nothing in return.

Hypersensitive to this issue of abandonment, and feeling strongly committed to others once I'm involved in their lives, I work hard to stay in contact. Needless to say, the volume of my correspondence over the years has been staggering—not to mention my phone bills.

When I was in eighth grade my family moved to a small town where I went to public school for the first time because the Catholic school offered only the first three grades. Not only did I come home spouting different political views from my parents, but the Sisters with whom I taught Saturday catechism classes wanted me to enter their congregation right after eighth grade. They went so far as to tell my mother that if I didn't join the community then, she would be the one responsible for my losing my vocation. Although I was already sure I wanted to be a nun, I was not drawn to these stern Sisters, and the thought of leaving home to join them was frightening.

Mom, however, took the Sisters' warning very seriously. To safeguard my vocation, my parents decided to move our family four hundred miles north to Santa Rosa where there was a Catholic high school—and where I began my journey with the Ursulines.

Sister Bernard interviewed me as an incoming freshman at Ursuline High School and, as usual, my mother bragged of my intention to become a nun. When Sister Bernard started telling me how much I would like the Ursuline Sisters, I informed her that I was going to be a Franciscan. To that, Sister Bernard simply smiled and told me that Ursulines were Franciscan tertiaries, so I could be both if I entered the Ursulines. "No," I told her, "my mind is made up." As she offered that smile again, she wisely pointed out that many things could happen in four years—and they did.

I thrived in high school, and the dedicated women who taught me became more than ideals of radical living; they became real people that I could talk to and rely on and whose strength surrounded me through that exciting time of new horizons in my life. I was still madly in love with Saint Francis, but the Franciscan Sisters of my childhood were far away and the Ursulines were right there. While I did know some of the story of Saint Angela and Saint Ursula, what really hooked me was my relationships with these real women who were Ursulines. Whether teaching me the fine points of a basketball guard, the mysteries of life cycles, or the logic of geometric theorems, the Sisters fulfilled my need for caring relationships. They were there for me.

So with all the naive idealism of an eighteen-year-old, I entered the Ursuline novitiate in Santa Rosa in 1964, immediately after high school graduation; I plunged wholeheartedly into the "ways of perfection." When we received the habit as novices, we were also given new names symbolizing the new persons we were becoming. I was delighted. I didn't like the old me anyway, so I thought I could just be someone else of my own choosing. I was professed "Catherine Marie," and I loved the idea of modeling the new me after Catherine of Sienna, such a strong figure of a woman, even advising the popes of her day.

Decades later, middle-aged and much wiser, I found myself in our Generalate in Rome listening to an old American song about wanting to be a Kellogg's cornflake or an English muffin making the most of a toaster. The song's crazy lyrics struck a chord in me. It made me chuckle to think of all the ways I had fought against accepting who I am, trying so hard to be someone else, someone more acceptable—as if I could possibly leave myself behind. At least I had made a small beginning of accepting who I am by taking back my own name: Dianne, a goddess name and spelled uniquely!

Since then I have continued the journey of discovering and expressing my uniqueness, fighting the pressure to take my identity from externals. I have expanded my universe by avid reading, diverse workshops, and enjoying art, theater, travel, and people. As a teacher I have loved experimenting, seeing new possibilities in modular scheduling, open classrooms, multimedia, and simulation games. I have gone from the traditional habit of my early religious life to colorful clothing accented by dangling earrings. In Montana, I'm identified as the nun who wears cowboy boots!

Throughout my religious life, the boundaries of my inadequacies have been pushed to new limits. In my early novitiate training, for example, I was given the position of senior novice so that I might "develop my leadership." Then there was the band in which everyone had to play an instrument— the fact that we couldn't read music and had no idea what we were doing seemed immaterial. During the precious free time I had, I would go out into the hills, as far from human ears as possible, to practice the coronet until sound, at least, came forth on command. I don't know who hated those practice sessions more, me or the cows.

When we wrote and performed a covenant play in the novitiate, I was given the part of Moses with two solo singing parts—although both the novice directress and I thought I couldn't do it. At least I could totally identify with this Moses character who stammered and stuttered that he couldn't do what God asked. Though at times I still stammer and think things are beyond me, I have worked hard, not to be Moses, but to be the best Dianne I can be.

My challenges to be all I could be continued to unfold after I graduated from college. My first assignment was in the Santa Rosa community: a group of retired Sisters and high school teachers, many of whom had taught me. Although I knew Ursuline Sisters as teachers, I had never thought much about the eventuality of my facing a classroom full of students. At the convent I was the girl they all knew so well, come home as a nun; at school I was the brand-new teacher to be tested. I felt like a child again.

While waiting for the school year to begin, I was asked to assist Sister Francis Connell with her kidney dialysis at home—another challenge. Although Sister Francis had been in charge of the boarders during my high school years, I didn't really know her and, in fact, I was in awe of her reputation as a courageous missionary in Alaska. Add to that the fact that I never wanted to be a nurse, it's small wonder that the first time I saw the dialysis machine I almost passed out. I tried to reason with my superior, explaining that I had none of the necessary training in dialysis. No matter; I was just an extra pair of hands. Sister Francis would tell me what to do as we went along.

Although I had witnessed the initial procedure of a dialysis run, I had never watched the finish. My first morning on the job, I was carefully pumping air at a consistent pressure into the tubing to force all Sister's blood back into her veins, when I happened to look up and notice that she was unconscious. I had no idea what was supposed to happen next. By some act of God, Sister Francis came to, just in time to close off the tubing before I pumped air directly into her veins. I was numb for weeks, thinking about how close I came to killing Sister Francis that very first day.

Through the years, if there was a crisis that could arise with the kidney machine, it did. One night the surgically inserted plastic tube in Sister Francis' vein popped out, even though doctors had assured us this never happened. Trying to keep Sister from bleeding to death, I discovered that she was unconscious when I heard someone scream that she was dead. I shouted back that she couldn't be dead—and God must have agreed with me; Sister recovered.

Women like Sister Francis, with her fierce tenacity for life, taught me more about Angela Merici, who founded the Ursulines, than all the research put together. Sister Francis was the mother figure of my religious life, passing on to me her legacy: a zest for life, missionary fervor, serious commitment laced with humor, and a deep love for community. Like Angela Merici before her, Sister Francis kept each of us engraved on her heart. I am able to love more because I knew and loved Sister Francis.

Each new ministry assignment was a bigger challenge than the previous one, but by my ninth year of teaching, I began to worry about getting in a rut. I had taught at our affluent high school in Santa Rosa and at our inner city, racially mixed high school in San Francisco.

Deeply involved in the lives of my students, I struggled with my desire for community—community that was not isolated from the people I served. Although we Ursulines have a long tradition as both educators and contemplatives, our history of monastic practices kept us separated from the world.

Wearing the habit set us apart while in the world, as did our cloister rules that prohibited us from sharing a meal or visiting a home. The school and convent were our world. But I wanted to be immersed in the lives of my students and their families, as well as in the lives of my Sisters.

Knowing my struggle, the provincial offered a suggestion, cautioning me not to laugh until I had heard her out. Yet when she suggested I go to our boarding school in Alaska, I burst into gales of laughter. I couldn't see myself living in Bush Alaska—too rugged for this Santa Rosa girl who loved to socialize. But the idea of a wider horizon attracted me and, within three days, I made up my mind to go.

A few months later my plane jolted to a stop on the packed dirt runway of the tiny local airport. I was collected in the mission truck and bounced along the six-mile stretch to the village and on to the school. Saint Mary's High School was a Jesuit and Ursuline mission with an illustrious history as an exemplary educational facility for Eskimo and Indian students, whether they went on to higher studies or returned to their villages as leaders. The Jesuit Volunteer Corp made up the majority of the staff at the school, along with Sisters, Brothers, and priests. Most of the students and all of the staff lived at the mission—where I was to get my wish to be immersed in people's lives.

With nine years of solid teaching experience, I felt a sense of professional competence while in a classroom setting. But Alaska was different: I was assigned as principal of the high school. I did not see myself as being organized enough for administration, and I had no idea how challenging teacher supervision would be since ninety percent of our volunteer teachers had no teaching experience and few role models to learn from. My work was cut out for me.

Saint Mary's, Alaska 1979, was so different from anything I had experienced. Used to California freeways and East

Coast beltways and turnpikes, I keenly felt the isolation of living in a locale that was accessible only by air. An hour jet flight northwest of Anchorage, Saint Mary's was on the Andreafski River, near the Yukon, with a population of two or three hundred people, depending on whether the boarding school students were there or not. There was nothing picturesque about the rutted dirt road from the airport to the village, nor about the dump that was the landmark between the town and the mission. Although I had seen photos of the mission, I was not prepared for the reality of a huge building made of corrugated tin. From affluent Santa Rosa, California—to that! My lessons in life began in earnest.

Being a competent professional was necessary, but being down to earth with people was essential. As I would sit in my office trying to get paperwork under control, Eskimo students regularly wandered in and out. I would drop what I was doing, give them my full attention, and ask what I could do to help. "Nothing, Sister," the students would respond. "We just want to come and sit!" Eager to help, I was initially deflated by this response, but soon learned that in this isolated part of the world, "being" was far more important than "doing." The students would sit and look at photos or yearbooks or whatever was around—anything that occupied their interest. Occasionally they asked questions or made requests—often they said nothing.

The Alaskan Bush was a place of sheer honesty where survival was a daily concern. Pretense had no place in that demanding environment. The children were on a first-name basis with the most ancient Elder, and no question was too personal to ask, no comment was too blunt to make. If you hadn't faced yourself before, you came to grips in Alaska where there were no props and few distractions.

Small wonder that I found those Ursuline missionaries to be a different breed altogether: independent, individual! The superior had her hands full with that crowd. Community life was not always easy with ten powerful woman together in the same house and school. Clashes were frequent—but laughter predominated. In those pioneer women, who took hardships in stride and lived intensely with and for the people, I saw anew what it means to be a daughter of Saint Angela.

Coming from the farmlands of California and loving the ocean, I thought I was quite attuned to the rhythms of nature, but Alaska opened my eyes in a whole new way of relating with the natural world. At Saint Mary's people lived off what the land provided naturally, so I learned both a self-sufficiency and a dependence that were closely intertwined. I reaped what God planted: wild cranberries, leaves for "tundra tea," green willow for smoking food, white fish in winter, salmon in the summer.

Life was fragile in that rugged land. Nature fed us, but could just as easily kill us. Survival depended on observation and careful planning because a change in weather could mean sudden death. Because there were no law enforcement officers and no rescue teams, violence was common. We had to depend on ourselves and one another to maintain a peaceful and healthy quality of life.

My first Thanksgiving in Alaska I went tent camping with a Sister who was far more experienced in wilderness survival than I. Although our intention was to be gone overnight, a blizzard trapped us and left us no choice but to stay put until the weather cleared—which took several days. A search party set out to look for us but turned back until the storm was over.

Although the tent and sleeping bags gave us shelter and warmth, by the second night the tent began to collapse and I thought I was going to die. When I wept with fear and misery, my companion yelled at me for getting emotional. When she invited me to patiently and calmly wait out the storm, I whined that my mother would kill me if I died because she thought I was crazy to go to Alaska in the first place. "You'll be dead anyway, so your mother won't kill you," Sister quipped.

We survived, although I was weak with dehydration by the time I got back to the mission. I returned from the experience with a new respect for both the power of nature and the strength of the human spirit. I also gained a deeper understanding of the strength and courage of Ursuline missionaries.

Although alcoholism was a major problem at Saint Mary's, and throughout the Alaska Bush for that matter, I dealt with its effects only at arms length. Students with repeated alcohol offenses were sent home, and since it was a boarding school, there was little interaction with parents. When I left Alaska four years later, however, I did not leave alcoholism behind.

I moved to Montana and began pastoral ministry at Saint Dennis Church in the town of Crow Agency on the Crow Indian Reservation, where another Ursuline Sister and I assisted the parish priest. There I came face to face with severe alcoholism on a daily basis. We lived in a large prefab house near the church, the train tracks, and the highway. We weren't far from the center of town, which consisted of a post office, two small grocery stores, a hamburger shack, and a tobacco shop with gambling machines.

Living among the people on the Crow Reservation, I found it impossible to keep the problem of alcoholism at bay. For many, out-of-control drinking lead to fighting, fatal accidents, physical and sexual abuse, including incest and sometimes murder. Bailing someone out of jail, providing a safe haven for someone afraid to go home, or just listening to a tale of woe was routine in our ministry.

At the end of my second year, my coworker moved to another ministry and, for the first time, I lived alone, more than an hour's drive from my nearest community of Ursuline Sisters. I also learned that a new pastor would be assigned to our parish—a man, by reputation, who was an active alcoholic and notoriously dysfunctional. Suddenly I was in abject dread, hoping that something—anything—would happen to stop that person from coming into the Crow community. The intensity of my dread was a clear indication that I had some unfinished business of my own to attend to. I entered counseling and, for the first time in my life, faced the alcoholism and dysfunction in my own family. I began my own process of recovery: learning to make healthy choices about work, responsibilities, boundaries, and feelings. I started to learn about taking care of my own needs.

Although I experienced a lot of pain in that inner work, I was in the midst of one of the greatest blessings of my life. Like Saint Paul, I learned that in my weakness is my strength. When two kids with sticky hands and runny noses crawled all over my house tearing the place apart, and their mother sat nervously on my sofa searching for the words to do her Fifth Step inventory of life with me, I could share some of my own story of recovery. I knew the shame of keeping the family secret and of battling the manipulations; I could be one with her—and others—enmeshed in an alcoholic environment.

Sometimes I became discouraged as I watched women put up with abuse and bad treatment on the reservation. As I thanked God for the regular support of my Alanon group, I gradually realized that my own local religious community was suffering a similar dysfunction. Because we were women religious, we were not in the habit of facing psychological problems or alcohol abuse within our own ranks. Instead, we were masters at accepting painful situations and hurtful behaviors as the way things had to be. Acceptance, after all, was culti-vated as a virtue.

How could I begin to counsel others toward healthy deci-sions in their lives if I was not doing my own work to learn healthy behaviors in the midst of an unhealthy community situation? So began the community's yearlong preparation for an alcohol intervention, and the mutual support necessary through a Sister's alcohol treatment. Unfortunately our ef-forts were temporary and within a year the community was back in denial.

Determined to continue healthy choices for my own life—risking rejection and judgment in the process—I decided to leave my local community.

That decision was the beginning of an ongoing process for me, a struggle to be a compassionate presence in the lives of people without falling into the trap of trying to change them or take responsibility for them, responsibility that is not mine to take. I practiced breaking that habit in the Crow community with a pastor who didn't always follow through on his responsibilities, and I succeeded to a certain degree. Such lessons are hard to learn, but the learning changes life dramatically.

My relationship with Sister Pat at Saint Mary's changed me forever. When I arrived in Alaska in 1979, I became friends with her, at least from my vantage point. Pat believed that she would be lucky to find even one real friend in her lifetime and considered all of us only acquaintances of one degree or another. I was hooked. If I could just be good enough, try hard enough, I could prove to be that real friend. Perhaps I had not been successful with my father, but Pat presented another impossible situation in which I might try again—harder this time.

Pat and I had many good times together. There was many a camping trip when we sat around a fire in the snow half the night talking. She taught me how to set a net for subsistence fishing, and under her instruction, I became an expert header and gutter. I survived both her temper and the fighting of the sled dogs. I knew I had really arrived the day Pat told me that I could hitch up the dog team and take them out by myself, the only music in the silence being the slurred swish of the sled runners.

But there were awful times too, times when Pat's wall would go up and I was left well outside her affections. I would try hard to break through and be there for her, but would end up getting hurt instead. Sometimes I could hardly believe how cruel Pat could be and, more amazingly, how I would put up with it.

A couple of years after I left Alaska, I got a call from Pat; she had just been diagnosed with cancer and was scheduled for surgery. Would I come up to Anchorage? I went, of course.

When I got to the hospital, I found a different Pat. Grappling with life-and-death choices, Pat was admitting her need for people for the first time in her life. At Thanksgiving Mass back in the village, Pat told the people her decision to fight for a longer life, not "outside," where she could get better care, but right there in the village that had been her home for more years than not. She told the people that they were her family and that she would be depending on them. No one had ever heard her talk like that. I sobbed to see the beautiful change in her—not a change that I had brought about, but one that only God and Pat could have made.

Months later when Pat learned that her chemotherapy had been unsuccessful, she called again asking me to come and help her die. She wanted to stay in the village, die at home, and be buried in the traditional Eskimo way. She actually apologized for asking such a difficult thing of me, especially while I was still mourning the recent death of Sister Francis. I didn't give it a second thought, of course. I had to go. My mother and several friends warned me that it might be more than I could do—caring for a dying person single-handedly in the middle of nowhere, with no medical assistance for God knows how long! I never wavered with my decision, however.

At Mass in San Francisco on Palm Sunday, I received word that Pat was in the Indian Health Hospital in Bethel. I knew she'd never go there if she had a choice; this was serious. I spent the entire day at the airport running from one ticket counter to another, getting on standby lists and waiting. Only three standbys were called for the last flight to Seattle; I was fourth on the list—yet I left on that plane. One of the three must have given up and left.

Nothing prepared me for how I found Pat when I arrived in Bethel. She was already drugged with morphine, looking like a swollen zombie. Knowing her wishes, I whisked her out of the hospital to a friend's private plane, and we headed for the village—for home. Pat lived three more days, and all that time her house was filled with people talking, eating, storytelling, laughing, and caring. I sat by her bed, holding her hand or wiping her forehead, hoping that in these last moments she would know how much she was loved. Her grip on my hand was so tight that when Father came to give her the sacrament of anointing, I had to pry her fingers away.

At one point a nurse friend took me into the bathroom, the only available spot for a private chat, and reminded me of my duty to help Pat die. Pat was stubbornly holding on to life, Mary said, and I was unconsciously encouraging her to hang on. Whenever Pat's breathing was slow to come, I would squeeze her hand, without even realizing it, reminding her to breathe. Mary was blunt about my responsibility to help Pat let go of life. Although I argued that I simply could not do it,

Mary insisted that I had no choice; I had accepted the task, and I owed it to Pat.

Suddenly in the middle of the night, I knew it was time to do something. I began to talk to Pat about letting go, about going home to God. I talked on and on, repeating over and over how Jesus was coming for her, how all she had to do was take his hand—perhaps believing those words myself for the first time; you don't say something to a dying person that you don't really believe. My belief at that moment was strong; I assured Pat that going home to God would be wonderful—and as I said the word *wonderful*, Pat died.

In that moment of death, Pat's face lost all the puffy strangeness of sickness and became translucent and beautiful. I've never seen anyone transformed like that. For days I had been struggling with all sorts of doubts, thinking my faith so weak. At the moment of Pat's death, I knew I was in the presence of God. I didn't see God's face, but I saw Pat see God's face. It was, indeed, *wonderful*.

Being with Pat through her struggle with cancer and death changed me forever. There are moments of regret—things I wish I had done during Pat's last year of life—but I had made a conscious caring decision to let the people of the village be there for her. Without trying to change Pat or take over her life, I had been able to be there for her when she needed me and to walk with her to the door of eternity.

From preparing Pat's body for burial to closing the house and gifting villagers with her possessions, the grieving process enriched me. One day as I was sorting through Pat's things, I found her profession ring. Instinctively, I slipped it on my finger with a promise to show to others the love and caring that Pat could not. Later that day a wise woman came for tea and we talked of Eskimo ways. She told me about the belief that the spirits of the dead live on, not only in the first child born and named for them after their death, but also in the persons who were with them at the moment of death and who prepared their bodies for burial. I cried, realizing the privilege that had been mine. In that warm exchange, I began my process of letting go. By the time I left Alaska, Pat was there no more, but I carried her in my heart. Her life, her hurts, and her struggles remain with me today and remind me of the transforming power of God's love.

As I write this, I am serving in one of my province's retirement houses; in the last three years, I have buried four of our Sisters. In each case I have had to face the decision of prolonging life or stopping treatment—a gut-wrenching experience. If I had not experienced something of letting go and trusting God with Pat, I would not be able to walk with these women the last years and days of their lives.

Looking back over the years, I realize that in my inadequacy I have lived from strong convictions: trying to be there for people. Wherever I was, I created a warm, inviting environment where people could gather in peace and comfort. As a teacher I fashioned colorfully creative learning spaces out of a lunch room, a glassed-in breezeway, and a tiny gym bathroom. My various offices were filled with plants, posters, books, games, photographs, once even a parakeet, and always people. While I served as a principal, my office was hardly a place one dreaded; rather, it was a comfortable hangout for student and teacher alike.

I have always loved to gather people together: family pool parties, volunteer reunions, student slumber parties and retreats, and even a Wild Boar party. My youngest brother gave me a whole smoked boar for Christmas one year, so I had to invite enough people to eat it. Friends are still talking about the wild gathering of folks who didn't even know one another but had such a great time together.

When I celebrated my silver jubilee a few years ago, I knew it had to be just such a crazy gathering. A formal Mass and fancy dinner was just not me. In fact, years earlier I had warned the Sisters that my jubilee would be at the ocean, but I don't think they took me seriously—that is, until the invitation arrived stating that the jubilee Mass and picnic would be held at Goat Rock Beach. A wonderful conglomeration of folks gathered on the beach that day, sat in a huge circle in the sand for Mass, and shared reflections after the Scripture readings with the ever-present sound of waves as music. It wasn't just my celebration, but a joyous recalling of how all our lives had been touched and blessed by God in one another.

Living on the Crow Reservation was the first time that I, as a nun, lived in a regular house instead of an institution. I loved having my own home: decorating for the seasons, baking bread and cookies, and having loads of company.

Whenever I think of the word *home*, my mom's cookie jar is the image that comes to mind. When we were children, Mom's cookie jar was the first stop for all our friends who thought those cookies were to die for. As we grew older, we realized that, yes, our friends did love the cookies, but they also gathered in the kitchen to get Mom's ear. She was both a good listener and a woman of great common sense. Over the years Angela Merici has become another such model for me. Her presence drew people together, healed differences, and gave people the support and encouragement they needed. That's how the Ursulines began, as a small company of women gathered around Angela.

In my own home I try to create just such a warm, comfortable space for people to be themselves with me. The scenes are as varied as the guests: a crowd playing a game or working a jigsaw puzzle, a family daring to sample Chinese stir-fry for the first time, little ones decorating bread bunnies for Easter, a mob having a birthday picnic and water fight in the yard, or folks having a long talk or a good cry. It's a welcoming home; all who enter are my family.

On Thanksgiving Day 1989, my last year at the Crow community, a family invited me to join them for dinner at the parish hall. In the midst of the celebration, I was formally adopted by one of the matriarchs and gifted with beaded moccasins, medallion, earrings, and a dance shawl. It was an intimate family gathering (of more than a hundred) to welcome me into their midst. One of the speakers noted that since I was now a member of the Bad War Deeds clan, I had a good excuse for acting a bit crazy, as everyone knows how daring Bad War Deeds people are.

About a month later my Crow mother died, and I mourned with my family. On my next birthday my Crow sister, Gladys, surprised me with a party, and a clan aunt, Clara, was asked to gift me with my Crow name. I was touched deeply by this because I respected Clara as the holiest elder on the reservation. My Crow name translates as Well Recognized Voice, and Clara explained to me later that the name came to her in a dream, symbolizing that, like Samuel in the Scriptures, I was called and responded, "Here I am, Lord." My voice was well recognized among the people as a messenger of the gospel.

Because "naming" has been significant in my ongoing acceptance of myself, I was concerned that receiving a new name might be a superficial, disappointing experience. Instead it was a profound and holy moment for me, epitomizing my vocation as a person, as a religious woman, as a follower of Angela. I feel strongly about my call to "be there" for people—understanding, supporting, and encouraging. I have grown into a stronger voice with sometimes a radical message, but always a familiar, comfortable presence.

As I look to the future, I know I want to continue "being there" as a healthy presence rather than an expression of my own neediness. In my process of self-discovery, I have come to realize that the lack of a relationship with my father has had a powerful impact on my life. Here I was a grown woman still ashamed that my father was not much of a father to me, hiding the fact that he didn't even speak to me for many years. Beginning with that experience, I plunged into many relationships in which the other was not capable of being there to the degree I wanted. Today I try to concentrate on gently doing my inner work without doing violence to myself, all the while exploring the wrecks of the past without blame or shame.

One of the lasting insights that hit me during my tertianship in Rome in 1990 was the profound realization that each of us is God's work of art, a priceless original! Since art has been a great love of my life, I think I finally understand something important in this metaphor. Everyone does not have to acclaim a piece of art for it to be a masterpiece; I do not need everyone's approval and love to be who I am, to glory in who I am: God's beloved.

As I roamed many of Europe's finest museums, I experienced a marvelous variety of masterpieces. I recall how taking pleasure in one treasured work did not detract from enjoyment of the next. Some became old friends that I revisited time and again—like the breathtaking Winged Victory of Samothrace in the Louvre—but I did not value others any less because of these favorites.

At one point, I realized that while I loved a beautifully sculpted piece of stone, I hated one of the Sisters in my tertian group. Yes, hated! No big reason, no previous experience; I just really hated her. When I finally confessed this to my spiritual director, I sobbed with enormous shame for having to use that dreaded word *hate*. After all, my life is supposed to be based on loving everyone. Yet there were masterpieces in every museum that did not really touch me, but whose value was not diminished in the least. As I reflected on this, I found my feelings for that particular person actually became less intense.

Early that year, as we were preparing for our thirty-day retreat, I admitted to my spiritual director that I was concerned about spending a concentrated period of time alone with God: "What if I don't know God anymore? What if there is no real relationship?" Father Ed joked with me and did his best to assuage my panic.

My first thirty-day retreat in the novitiate had been a horrible experience of desolation and temptation. Perhaps I was too young to handle such intense experiences of prayer. But that was the experience of a young, inexperienced novice. As a middle-aged religious approaching silver jubilee, I was ripe for the experience of what can only be described as sheer intimacy. A father image of God has never been helpful for me, so I adopted a feminist approach to God as Mother, as Creator. Who would have imagined that at that point in my life God would take to calling me "little girl" and that I would weep at the tenderness. It proved to be a monthlong honeymoon with God who kept repeating: "I've known since you were a little girl that you would be mine."

Jealously I guarded our time together—God and me—and it was wonderful. As I sat on the balcony outside my retreat room with my feet propped on the wrought iron railing, meditating on John the Baptist, I had what can only be described as a mystical moment. God spoke to me as clearly as any conversation I've ever experienced: "I want to so fill your horizon that you see everything through me, through my eyes." Without a flicker of hesitation, the plaintive question popped out of me: "Will you be there?" To which God repeated: "Through my eyes." I wept with joy!

My horizons have been continually broadened by my life experiences and, while those horizons now stretch farther than the eye can see, I know with surety that they are so filled with God that I am actually breathing in God's very essence wherever I am and in whatever I am doing. I need not search frantically for someone to "be there" for me because God is that Someone. We are one in a way I never thought possible. Once a long time ago I noticed that when I pray, my hands need to touch something: the words on the page of Scripture, the earth, the wood of the pew, a blade of grass, the follicles of a feather. I need to stay in touch, so God can so fill my horizon.

A Pilgrim Path

SUSAN BREMER, OSU

Since we are surrounded by this cloud of witnesses...
persevere in running the race which lies ahead;
let us keep our eyes fixed on Jesus,
who inspires and perfects our faith

—HEBREWS 12:1-2

Nothing highlights the fragility of life more immediately or more acutely than a life-threatening illness. As one jolted into reality by the discovery of a lump and a subsequent diagnosis of cancer, I can surely attest to that fact. My life, sure and strong for forty years, became fragile in an instant. And I, who had always been so self-sufficient, was suddenly vulnerable and needy.

I made the discovery in January 1993. Not prone to panic or hysteria, I considered the likely possibility that the lump was merely a cyst, and I decided to wait it out. Several weeks later, the lump remained. Still not totally grasping the potential gravity of the situation, I went for a mammogram. Before I had the chance to flee the office, the radiologist had my doctor on the phone. He, in turn, asked to speak with me.

"Sister," he said, "I'm afraid we have a problem." I had read similar dialogue in novels and had heard it in B-grade movies, but never gave it serious thought. It's fiction, after all. In my wildest dreams, I never expected it to happen that way—and certainly not to me.

The lump was large and irregular in shape. When the doctor said it didn't look good, I was dumfounded. As he continued to speak, calmly reciting names of surgeons at various hospitals, the conversation took on a rather surreal cast. And in that life-altering instant, time stood still.

I hung up the phone, remembered to thank the nurse (my convent training), and left the office. I stopped in the lobby to call Kathleen, one of the Sisters with whom I was living. True friend that she is, Kathleen had wanted to accompany me to my appointment, but I had made light of the situation and politely refused her offer. There I was, at a pay phone in a building a mere ten-minute drive from home, calling to tell her my news. I think I needed to speak the words out loud to grasp their full meaning. Seconds later, after dropping my bomb, I hung up, knowing that tears would be my companion on the drive home.

The typical blur of activity that surrounds illness and hospitalization began: a visit to the surgeon for a needle aspiration that, while inconclusive in determining malignancy, identified "highly suspicious" cells; preadmission testing; a combined biopsy and mastectomy procedure. Unlike my doctor, I went into surgery with a glimmer of hope that the lump would prove benign. I awoke from surgery, looked up into the face of a dear friend and groggily asked, "Did they do it?" "Yes," she whispered, "it's gone." That was that.

Of the many lymph node samples taken, only one showed evidence of cancer invasion; that was the good news. Only one, however, is enough to warrant chemotherapy; that was the bad news. Nausea, hair loss, dry mouth, hot flashes, trips to the hospital emergency room: for six months I endured them all. There were many dark moments—far worse than the initial diagnosis and surgery—when fear and discouragement threatened my well-being. Losing my hair was a hellish, frightening experience.

With each washing, for example, my hair grew thinner and the part grew wider. When I could no longer bear to touch it, Kathleen gently washed and combed it for me. Finally, four weeks after my first treatment, and two weeks after the initial fallout, my hair was completely gone; I was bald. Within another month I lost my eyebrows and the long lashes that had been my pride and joy and the envy of my friends. Each time I faced myself in the mirror, it was a shock. Still, once the hair loss was complete, I was relieved. The worst was behind me; new growth, new life, could begin.

The journey from diagnosis through treatment was one of ups and downs. Happily, the ups were more plentiful. I never questioned *Why me?* Rather, I thought, *Why not me? Why should I be exempt?* Besides, my part of the ordeal was, in a very real sense, the easier one. The actual physical pain was minimal, and I never seriously doubted that I would recover. I can't say the same for my family and friends. Each time I saw them, their faces belied their fears for my life and their own suffering born of helplessness.

Many times a day I prayed in thanksgiving for my mother and father and for the sense of humor they had given me. My own ability to find the lighter side of the situation seemed to enable my family and friends to do the same. There were tasteless jokes about double-breasted suits, and one Ursuline friend, trying to encourage me through my balding process, quipped, "Don't think of it as losing hair; think of it as gaining face." Yes, laughter is indeed a potent and powerful medicine whose curative powers have never failed me.

When I finally recovered from the curse of chemotherapy side effects, I found myself wanting to write about my ordeal. My musings stemmed not from a need to remember the illness, but from a need to remember the value of life, to remember to cherish life, to remember to savor its goodness. I celebrate life today because of all those who helped me through yesterday's trial and pain and fear.

I am fortunate, indeed, for in the midst of terrible darkness, I came face to face with the Almighty. No, I never truly feared for my life, never had visions of death's bright light beckoning me home. But in the people who rallied around me, I experienced myself wrapped in a blanket of love and encouragement that would not tolerate even a hint of giving up or giving in. Through them, I experienced the tender and compassionate love of God.

My family and non-Ursuline friends provided wonderful support. Deluged with flowers and cards, I was humbled and overwhelmed by their outpouring of love and concern. But it was my Ursuline friends and Sisters who walked with me through each day: my housemates, Kathleen, Ann Patrick, and Colette, who so lovingly shared my burden and celebrated each of my homecomings; Pam, nursing director of our infirmary, who served as my personal caregiver and spirit booster; all of the nuns with whom I work and pray and play. I give special credit and gratitude to all the elderly and infirm Sisters who prayed me back to health and wholeness; they were the true miracle workers.

The experience of illness was obviously a significant event for me. Now, three years after concluding treatments, I look back with amazement that something of such consequence actually happened to me, and that I survived it well. Actually, I have come to count my intimacy with cancer as a time of profound grace and blessing in my life.

My experience opened my eyes to the urgency of women's health issues. As a result, I have the voice to speak to others about attending to their own physical well-being. It has also opened my heart to those similarly afflicted. Since my surgery, I have been an active participant in a breast cancer support group. At first, when the invitation to join was extended, I resisted. *I am coping remarkably well*, I thought—and I already had a built-in support system. But I relented, and have been a regular ever since. Naturally, I began on the receiving end of the support system, but now find myself acting as cheerleader and encourager. I speak readily of my triumph and offer my new head of hair as a sign of hope to those newly come.

Within this sacred gathering we have forged a bond of true sisterhood. We rejoice with one voice; we grieve with one heart. We share our stories again and again, conscious of their deeper meaning, their power to soothe and to heal. Over time, each person's tears of anguish are mysteriously transformed and redeemed, becoming the stuff of hope and a wellspring of thanksgiving.

A similar bond exists within my Ursuline family, among those of us who have dared to speak of our common experience. I recall the blessing of one Sister survivor who contacted me after my surgery; her story of recovery, practical advice about wigs and make-up, and promise of prayers gave me courage and strength. In the past three years, I have tried to respond in kind to others facing the same experience. I find that reaching out is sometimes difficult, not because I hesitate, but because the time-honored veil of secrecy still exists, particularly among women religious. We converse so easily about our work or the movie we saw last week; we can discuss the latest views on community life or the deplorable state of the world. But we are so hesitant to speak of our inner selves or the burdens we carry. How terribly sad that is. How much easier it would be to deal with cancer—with all of life's harsher moments—if we were willing to break open our lives and our pain. I am grateful for the few brave souls who have dared to break the silence to reach out to me and others. Together we form a channel of support that, for me, has become a chain of blessing.

Put into a broader context, my experience of illness is but

another stop on the larger journey of life that offers me a unique lens for review and reinterpretation. The journey itself has been a pilgrimage, more than four decades in the making, marked by highways and valleys and many blessedly boring plains. It is a road lined with faces—some shadowy and nameless, others vivid and clear—of fellow pilgrims who graced my path for a time, then moved on—or away. It is, finally, a story of faith and family.

I was born on November 11, 1952, in East Cleveland, Ohio, the third of four children of Paul and Loyola Bremer. With sisters Joanne and Joyce, three and four years older respectively, and a brother, Jeff, who followed five years later, there was always plenty of activity in our house. While not perfect and utopian as the Andersons of *Father Knows Best* fame, neither did our family portrait resemble the crude, battle-scarred TV clan of Roseanne Arnold.

Money was scarce and, like many families, we had our share of problems and dysfunction. Years later, I would look back and marvel at my mother's quiet acceptance of it all and her amazing wizardry with money. She rivaled the best on Wall Street in juggling funds, frequently "robbing Peter to pay Paul," just managing to elude the bill collectors. Still, living as we did from one paycheck to the next, with money running out before the week did, we never felt deprived, even on birthdays and holidays.

Somehow, Christmas was always magical. Mom was never extravagant or frivolous in spending, but she bent over backwards to accommodate our simple wish lists. It might not have been the pricier brand name or the exact item, but it always came just close enough to delight. There was a time during my adolescence when mohair sweaters were popular and oh how I wanted one. So naturally, as Christmas neared, I noted it at the top of my list. On Christmas morning I opened a package tagged for me. No, it was not exactly the sweater of my dreams, but the label stated that it was, indeed, mohair—at least fifteen percent. Mom sat there smiling, so pleased to have granted my wish. You couldn't help but love her.

Loyola Angela Corrigan Bremer was a woman of simple, yet remarkable faith. (Given her unusual baptismal name, it helped that she was also possessed of a wonderful sense of humor.) She was, without a doubt, the greatest grace of my life, introducing me to God and sowing the seeds of faith. Her God, thankfully, was a far cry from the stern and distant God of the Catholic Church of that time; her God was loving and gentle and always near. So deeply ingrained in me was this notion of a loving God, that even as a child I was terribly saddened and troubled to learn that only Catholics would go to heaven. The God I believed in would never punish people just for being "Protestant." I remember crying one day when one of my playmates, also a Catholic, threatened to tattle on me for befriending a girl who was a Jehovah's Witness. She was nice; didn't that count for anything? An open, ecumenical heart was beating even then.

The relationship I shared with my mother was forged by the special times we shared. There was a wonderful period, when Joyce and Joanne were already in school and Jeff had not yet arrived on the scene, during which I had her all to myself. Our days were spent in spur-of-the-moment trips downtown or in the quiet of a library or art museum. Sometimes we would sneak off to Euclid Beach Park for a few stolen hours of excitement on the Thriller, the Racing Coaster, the Over the Falls, and the Bug. We watched game shows and planned exotic trips we were sure we would win—never mind that we never actually posted an entry form.

Mom and I had some marvelous times, but most special for me was attending Holy Week services together. From preschool age on, and through Mom's last Easter, I accompanied her to church for the triduum. From Holy Thursday morning to late Saturday night, we kept prayerful vigil, attending each liturgy and following each word and action outlined in the missal. The sense of mystery and solemnity moved me, and like the incense that marked each sacred day and ritual, God's presence settled upon us and held us in grace. Even today, when I participate in Holy Week liturgies with the catechumens whose journeys of faith I have shared, I think of those early days with Mom, and I whisper a prayer of thanksgiving.

When I came of school age, Mom confidently entrusted me to the care of the Ursuline nuns who had been doing a fine job with Joyce and Joanne at Saint Philomena School. The Ursulines came to Cleveland in 1850 and established the first school of the diocese. Since that time they opened more than thirty other schools and were greatly respected as educators and administrators.

I believe that in my heart I have belonged to the Ursulines since the day I met them, as a frightened six-year-old timidly entering Sister Ursula Marie's first-grade classroom. From that point on, I assumed the label "Ursuline born and raised." It was as simple—and as profound—as that.

Dotted with the usual childhood ups and downs, and the typically more dramatic ecstasies and tragedies of early adolescence, my school years passed quickly. I was truly blessed to have had so many fine Ursuline teachers, like Sister Gerard, who instilled in me a love of English and introduced me to the fine art of diagramming sentences—which also appealed to the math lover in me; like my high school math teacher, Sister Mary Antoine, whom I proudly proclaim to be the best teacher I ever had; like Sister Susan Liderbach who, in addition to Latin and religion, taught me to like myself. Some of the Sisters have since died and a few, like Susan, have left religious life. But all of them have left their mark on my life.

The Ursulines' influence far exceeded the realm of my intellectual or psychosocial development; it penetrated my heart and soul. As a teenager I recognized that the "mysterious" quality I had ascribed to the nuns as a child was more appropriately described as "graced confidence." There was a joyful, laughing spirit about them that attracted me, and a sense of peace and contentment that drew me in for a closer look.

My senior retreat gave birth to my Ursuline dream, as in prayerful reflection I considered my life as a nun. *Was God calling me? Was I holy enough? Could I give up my life for God? Yes—maybe—yes.* Afraid to trust my own inner voices, I sought the advice of an Ursuline confidante who, after hearing my story, encouraged me to follow my heart.

When I shared with my mother my wish to enter the Ursuline community, she was thrilled. I always knew of her pride in me, but this sent it soaring to new heights. She loved and respected the Ursulines as much as I did, so this was a variation of the proverbial "match made in heaven."

In April 1970, with a fair amount of excitement and an overabundance of stomach-churning anxiety, I faced my initial meeting with the Ursuline general superior. Mother Annunciata seemed at the time an imposing figure, though I'm sure now it was her position that intimidated me. As I recall, she told me something of the community's history, then asked a few questions about my family, about school, and about my desire to be an Ursuline. I rattled on nervously in reply, telling her about my retreat experience and about how I really wanted to be a journalist, but would consider being a teacher since that's what Ursulines did. I must have answered satisfactorily because after assuring me of her prayers and encouraging me to do the same, she sent me back to my parents who were waiting in the car—in and out in less than half an hour. I was as good as in.

During the last months of my high school career, I spent several weekends at the Ursuline mother house getting to know the novices and learning a little of what was in store for me. I found that I questioned much of what I saw: Why couldn't novices speak to professed Sisters? How could one person decide for an entire group what constituted fun and recreation? Much of it seemed rather silly and unnecessarily rigid, but my desire to be an Ursuline far surpassed my questioning. This was the life I wanted, and rules or no rules, I would have it. My entrance date was scheduled for the following January. In the meantime I was to begin studies at Ursuline College and prepare for convent life. All was well—or so I thought.

In December I was invited to the mother house for a weekend of meeting and getting to know the other four young women with whom I would be entering the following month. Much joking and laughter marked our time together, particularly the first night as we prepared for bed in the five-person dorm to which we'd been assigned. Left to ourselves we talked more openly about being there and about our nervousness. I enjoyed them—in varying degrees—and thought we would jell quickly as a group. Thoughts of jelling fell quickly from my mind the next day when I was presented with a decision for which I was not prepared and in which I had no voice.

During our stay, each of us met with the assistant novice directress, to tie up loose ends and make final preparations for the big day. When my turn came on Saturday afternoon, I entered the office with absolutely no inkling of what was to come. The directress began simply enough by asking how I was enjoying my stay and about how the group was getting along. Then, with no warning, her smile gave way to concern as she spoke of a letter she had received from one of my teachers. A lump formed in my throat and a sense of foreboding descended.

What followed was undoubtedly the most humiliating moment of my seventeen years, as phrases like "emotionally unstable" and "socially immature" flew from her mouth like darts, piercing me to the very core. In the end, her message was simple: owing to the letter she had received and now held in her hand, it was the community's opinion that I was not ready for religious life and, therefore, should delay my entrance.

I was stunned. Surely this couldn't be happening. What a sight I must have made as I begged and pleaded, practically throwing myself at the woman's feet. What would I tell my parents? Surely I couldn't tell them the truth. What would they think?

Somehow, I managed to resist the urge to bolt the premises, no doubt wanting to show that I was made of tougher stuff. Facing the novices and my newfound friends was difficult, realizing that they would be proceeding without me. The next day, as I stood waiting at the door for my parents, Sister James Francis, the formation directress, approached me. "I know nothing of what's happened this weekend," she said, "and I don't want to know. You are sad and hurt right now, but I want you to know one thing. If you are meant to be here, some day, by the grace of God, you will be, regardless of what anyone may say or do." Those words did little at the time to ease the ache in my stomach and heart, but the determination and truth they conveyed and the kindness with which they were offered found a permanent home within me. When I finally did enter ten years later, one of the first people to greet me was Sister James Francis. I don't know whether she even remembered her words; I never forgot them.

Meanwhile, I faced breaking the news to my parents. I formulated a plan: I would tell them during our drive home, but not until we were off the mother house property. Then, when the moment was right, I would calmly tell them that I—not the community—had decided to postpone my entrance. I rehearsed the words over and over, hoping to sound convincing.

Finally, when my father's car pulled into view, I grabbed my suitcase, ran down the stairs, ducked quickly into the car, and blurted out, "I'm not going. I've changed my mind." My carefully rehearsed announcement was quickly awash in a sea of tears. While my father drove in stunned silence, my mother, gently squeezing my hand, assured me that all would be well. I suppose we talked later about my alleged change of heart, but I never told her the real story. Being a mother, being my mother, she probably knew instinctively the truth that I couldn't admit, even to myself. When she died years later, one of my very first thoughts was, "My God, now she knows everything!"

I have always believed that each experience of life, no matter how painful or difficult, is an invitation to grow. That was no exception. The incident, still painful to recall more than twenty-five years later, was definitely a life shaper for me and invited me to deeper self-reflection. It's telling, I think, that my immediate reaction to news of the postponement was not to defend myself, but rather to worry about my parents' response. In the deepest part of me I was relieved. I guess I knew, as the letter's author had known, that I wasn't yet ready for such a step, and that had I entered, it most likely would have been a very short stay. While I believe it could have been handled better and with more expedience, I know that all involved acted in my best interest. Nonetheless, the plan I had laid out for myself came to a screeching halt, and I was directed to another path, one divinely ordained.

With the convent rejection behind me, I focused my energy and attention on continuing my studies at Ursuline College, the community's liberal arts college for women. Months earlier, believing an Ursuline teaching career to be in my future, I had declared myself a math/education major. With all thoughts of the convent on hold, I decided to abandon both math and education and switch to English. I was much happier in that field; my math teacher was happier too.

In October of my junior year, my family was devastated by the sudden death of my twenty-four-year-old sister. Joyce, who had been an outstanding student in high school, had found her way into a rough crowd after graduation, and was quickly initiated into the world of drugs. By the time my parents recognized what was happening, it was too late. By the age of twenty, Joyce was married—and addicted to heroin. Six months before her death she had entered a recovery program with an experimental drug. It was the methadone that killed her.

My parents were inconsolable. They loved Joyce, suffered with her throughout her addiction, and encouraged and supported her through each step of treatment. If there was any consolation to be found in the tragedy, it was that Joyce had tried, at least, to turn her life around. Sadly, the effort hadn't been enough.

Six months later, my grandmother died. Although elderly and infirm, she had remained an integral part of our family—and then she was gone. Life in the Bremer household appeared to be in a state of collapse. In a six-month period, I lost a sister and a grandmother; my mother lost a daughter and her mother.

My mother's remarkable faith was sorely tested. What faith could withstand such terrible sorrow? Hers did. Although there were many tears and countless days of anguished questioning, she never despaired, and never turned from the God she loved. There is a Scripture verse, a line from Saint Paul's Epistle to the Philippians, that has become my favorite, probably because it reminds me of my mother. "I can do all things through [God] who strengthens me" (4:13). I know Mom believed that; I watched her live it.

Throughout this difficult period we were bolstered by many wonderful friends, among them the Ursuline nuns who came en masse to offer condolences and promises of prayer. Marveling at the great number of Sisters at Joyce's wake, one family member remarked, "Is there a nun in the family we don't know about?" Certainly it was an overwhelming outpouring of love and support. Many of those who came had taught Joyce at Saint Philomena's or at Ursuline Sacred Heart Academy, and they wanted to share reminiscences of her from earlier, happier times. Some were my teachers at the college; others were the Sisters who lived in Saint Philomena Convent and who, for the past ten years, had been our neighbors and friends. They generously provided meals and stood ready to offer any needed assistance. We never forgot their kindness.

In May 1974 I graduated from Ursuline College with a degree in English. Unlike many of my friends, I managed to secure a job before the big day, so my celebration was two-fold. After a week of vacation, I began my career as an advertising copywriter. It wasn't Madison Avenue, but it would do; writing jobs were hard to come by. I was one of a corps of writers hired to create a travel and tourism program geared to the country's upcoming bicentennial. Seven months into the project, funding was withdrawn and the project was shelved. Our services were no longer required.

Although my stay had been short, I had enjoyed the work; losing the job was a great disappointment. Besides, Christmas was just around the corner. I considered my options: I could be sulky and Scrooge-like and create a "blue Christmas" for all or I could "deck the halls" and enjoy my extended "vacation." I chose the latter.

The house was filled with the customary hustle and bustle, and Mom, in typical fashion, dashed from store to store to complete her shopping. Accompanying her on one of her last Christmas Eve trips, I noticed she had trouble catching her breath, a frequent occurrence in her six-year bout with emphysema. By day's end, looking totally drained, she balked at the suggestion that we skip Midnight Mass. "I'll be okay," she insisted. "I just overdid it today. I'll be good as new in the morning."

With the first light of Christmas morning we awoke one by one and made our way to the living room to open presents. Mom joined us, coffee cup in hand, looking considerably better. Hours later, I was in the kitchen getting coffee, when she called to me from the bedroom where I found her curled up in bed, in considerable discomfort. Anticipating my lecture, she promised to see a doctor the next day. With Mom calling out directions and encouragement from her bed, Joanne and I fixed a fine Christmas dinner, but our celebration was far from festive.

By the next afternoon Mom was in the hospital, suffering from a bleeding ulcer caused by her emphysema medication. Discontinuing the drug helped the ulcer to heal, but it caused the emphysema to worsen considerably. When my father brought her home ten days later, he had an oxygen tank in tow with other equipment to follow.

Everything was happening much too quickly. Mom had never been sick, and there she was surrounded by all this machinery. Thinking back on that time, I scarcely can believe how nonchalantly I responded to such a dramatic turn in the life of one so important to me. Despite the losses we'd suffered as a family, I was a stranger to illness and hadn't a clue as to what was happening.

With Mom's illness looming larger and larger, the rest of us outlined a plan that put me in the position of primary caregiver. Several times each day, I helped Mom with the inhalation machine, as the technician had shown us, but with no apparent sign of improvement. As I spent more and more time with her in her bedroom, we talked and prayed and, in moments of her breathless frustration, we cried. We also laughed. Though neither of us spoke of it, I believe we both knew we were preparing for parting.

Mom's condition seemed to worsen, but she would not hear of going to her doctor any earlier than her next scheduled appointment. Early one morning we found her totally unresponsive, appearing unable to hear or speak or focus. Something was drastically wrong.

Mom was admitted to the hospital intensive care unit, badly dehydrated and with her lungs dangerously congested. These conditions, in turn, were taxing her heart. It didn't look good. The doctor encouraged us to go home to wait. Visiting hours for the ICU were several hours away.

At home we busied ourselves with anything to keep from thinking. While we alternated visits to the hospital, Dad made calls to alert family members to Mom's deteriorating condition. By the next evening, Mom's condition had been upgraded from poor to fair; an answer to our prayers. With significantly lighter hearts we made yet another round of phone calls, then settled down for some well-deserved popcorn and television.

When the phone rang shortly before eleven that Sunday night, we all froze. Being closest to the phone I answered. It was a nurse at the hospital asking to speak to my father. After listening a moment, he responded, "We'll be right there." An hour and a half later my mother was dead at the age of fifty-six. The sadness that gripped me was like nothing I had ever experienced, and most likely never will again. My mother, whose love, laughter, and faith had provided the bedrock of my life, was gone.

Hundreds of persons came to the funeral home to pay their respects. I was not alone in my admiration of this woman; clearly, others had experienced her goodness as well. How proud I was that night to be the daughter of Loyola Bremer.

Even now, more than twenty years after her death, she continues to inspire and guide me. When I seek counsel or when I am heavy-hearted, I cry out and she responds. Through a bonding of spirits that transcends even the grave, I can discern her unspoken words of wisdom and advice; even more wonderfully and mysteriously, at times, I can actually feel her presence. She has never abandoned me.

Just as my mother's life inspired my own, the experience of her death moved me forward on my journey of faith, ever closer to its real beginning. My lay-off from the advertising agency freed me to care for my mother, but that ministry came to an end. Miraculously, the next day—the morning after Mom's death—I received a call, inviting me back to work. I had always been a firm believer in providence, but that act of God's intervention amazed even me.

Within six months we finished the writing project, and I was again unemployed, but this time with a little more experience behind me. I applied and was hired as a proofreader at the Catholic Universe Bulletin, Cleveland's diocesan newspaper—and thus began some of the most wonderful years of my life.

In those days, a family-like closeness existed among the staff, and in that circle of easy friendship and camaraderie, the dismal surroundings of our chancery building office took on a comfortable, homey character. Lively debates about the

Church were daily fare and—as Catholics young and ancient, semiheretical and ultraconservative—we discussed and dissected all the news we covered "up close and personal." There were the back-to-back elections of Popes John Paul I and II, the ever-controversial Church teaching on birth control, and the declining numbers of priests and religious. The list went on and on. Though our railings and clever arguments never made it to print, the sharing of ideas and beliefs birthed in me a new enthusiasm for the Church I had always loved, not the Church of power and authority, but the authentic Church, the people of God.

Along the pilgrimage of my life, these were the plain years —no personal peaks or valleys, just quiet growth and contentment. They were years of growth for my family as well. My father's marriage to Isabell Macy, a widowed mother of three grown children, doubled the size of our family, while my brother's marriage to Isabell's daughter more than doubled everyone's confusion; stepsister and stepbrother becoming husband and wife, making Dad and Isabell both stepparent and in-law to each other's child. The unusual unions made great conversation starters; they also created a wonderful new family.

Within me, however, a gnawing, barely perceptible ache was growing. Since my convent plans were aborted, I banished all thoughts of habits and vows. At work, I still tossed out occasional threats of quitting to become a nun, but these generally followed my rantings on missed deadlines or disappointing romances. The ache within me prodded and kicked, unsatisfied by Sunday Mass and Communion, by charismatic prayer or Scripture study. The feeling had nothing to do with what I did, but everything to do with who I was and who I could be. I sensed an emptiness, but didn't know—or was afraid to admit—how to fill it. I needed a truth-speaker.

Sister Susan Mary was that truth-speaker for me, as she had been since high school. Having taught me in English class and directed me in musicals, this teacher-turned-friend knew me well—well enough to have recognized ten years earlier that I wasn't ready for the convent. She was the one who wrote the letter that kept me from joining the Ursulines. I had suspected as much at the time and upon confronting her then, she admitted to being the letter's author. That same day, after a tearful exchange about what had happened and why and how, we reconciled. And while we kept in touch through the years, we never spoke of the letter or the convent again.

All that changed one May evening in 1980 when I invited Susan Mary to my apartment for dinner. Enjoying after-dinner coffee and conversation about recent happenings in our lives, she stopped me short with a simple question. "What are you waiting for?" My puzzled expression urged her on. "When are you going to give in and do what God is calling you to do?" No other probing was needed. Like Saint Paul after his conversion, the scales fell from my eyes and I could see. She, who had once blocked my path to the Ursulines, invited me to come.

We talked long into the evening as Susan Mary answered each of my feeble excuses and objections, one by one. She assured me that I wouldn't have to give up my friends, nor would I have to be a teacher, and best of all, my previous file had been destroyed. At that point, I was out of excuses.

Later that night, I telephoned my sister in Oklahoma City to tell her my news; I knew she'd understand. "Susan Mary was here for dinner," I began, then added quickly, "and I'm going into the convent." (What an amazing contrast to the "I'm not going; I've changed my mind" declaration of an earlier time.) Joanne's momentary silence gave way to a rush of questions. How and when had I decided? How soon would I go? What did I need? We talked at length about what had happened that evening and about what lay ahead. Just as I anticipated, her excitement matched my own; in Joanne I had chosen the very best place to start for sharing my good news. And that night I knew, as I lay awake in my bed, that the time of real beginning had come.

Caught up in a whirlwind of excitement, I busily set about planning my summer and the remaining months of 1980. Four other women were preparing to join the community in August, and I had hoped to accompany them. Faced with the tasks of selling my furniture and closing up my apartment, however, and attending to the prerequisite physical, eye, and dental exams, there was too much to do. January 3 was set as my entrance date. But before proceeding further, I needed to tell the rest of my family and friends about my decision.

To boost my confidence and bolster my courage for facing my family, I first shared the news of my decision with my closest friends; they knew of my restlessness and would understand my desire to take such a step. They responded, as I knew they would, with joyful enthusiasm and support. I hoped my family would be as receptive. They weren't.

My father and Isabell were far from enthusiastic. "Didn't you try that once?" Dad asked. Stifling my frustration with Dad's unbelievably faulty memory, I explained that while I was close to entering years before, I hadn't actually done so. I tried to explain my decision, describing my feelings of emptiness and of wanting to do and be something more; I assured them that I was making the right choice for me. The slow nod of their heads gave a hint of assent, but clearly they were not convinced. We were spiritual strangers. They didn't know and couldn't understand the journey I had traveled and the step I longed to take. While good and faith-filled people in their own way, they just couldn't comprehend how I could choose life as a nun over that of a wife and mother. "We just want you to be happy." "I know," I responded, "and I will be."

With assurances of their love and support, I set out for January.

My journey to the Ursulines involved one more stop. Needing a thousand dollars to help finance my novitiate years, I had to give up my apartment and find another place to live. My options were limited: I could move in with my father and stepmother or find a friend with a big house. Instead, I found Bernie. At the time I didn't know Bernie very well, having met her only recently through another friend in my prayer group. Bernie heard of my plight and invited me to move in with her and her two sons, ages three and six. When no other solution surfaced, I gratefully—though hesitantly—accepted.

Throughout my six-month sojourn with the Harveys, we became best of friends. In Bernie I found not only a friend, but a sister and a soul mate whose faith and gentleness inspired my own. We shared histories of hurts and struggles, and in the telling, we were healed. In sharing prayer and faith, she helped me prepare interiorly for the convent, while I helped her care for her children. While I had come expecting to share household expenses, she wouldn't hear of it, so attuned was she to a gospel spirit of charity and so confident in God's bountiful providence. Bernie was a woman whose very life proclaimed God's goodness. In half a year's time, I enjoyed a lifetime of blessing.

One month before my scheduled entrance into their community, the Ursulines were devastated by the death of Sister Dorothy Kazel. On December 2, 1980, she and three missionary companions were brutally murdered by government forces in El Salvador. Never before had I witnessed such grief, as Sisters, old and young, wept openly in the hallways, brought face to face with the violence of a far-away land. For many days, the mother house was still, save for the movement of tears.

Suddenly my life seemed very small indeed. I was about to enter the convent, feeling rather smug about the "sacrifice" I was making—yet, what sacrifice? What did I know about sacrifice? The deaths of my former teacher and her companions suggested I knew very little. For perhaps the first time, I saw beyond the narrow confines of my life to another world, to a tiny country described by Dorothy as one "writhing in pain." In one moment of insanity, four voices were silenced, challenging the rest of us to take up the call.

I awoke on January 3, 1981, with a knot in my stomach; the day had come. Anxious as I was to begin my life as an Ursuline, my leave-taking of Bernie and the Harvey home was painful. Although confident in the lasting bond we had forged, that time of gift and grace was drawing to a close, leaving us poised on the edge of change and adjustment.

After spending the day with my parents, I rode with them to the mother house for the Mass that would serve as my official welcome into the Ursuline community. Upon crossing the threshold, I was greeted by Laura, a novice and friend. "Is that mascara you're wearing?" she roared in her best stage whisper. I was then whisked away for a phone conversation with general superior, Sister Bartholomew, who was at the time hospitalized with a back injury. She welcomed me warmly and assured me of her prayerful support.

Memories of the Mass are fuzzy, owing no doubt, to the myriad of emotions that gripped me the previous night. Who presided, what songs were sung, and what was said in the homily are lost to me, although in my mind I see vividly a kaleidoscope of faces—family and friends and Sisters—gathered with me there in the chapel to celebrate and to christen my journey. In that sacred moment and place, my life's paths and companions came together, linked both by the past and by the promise of the future.

I slid easily into Ursuline life and into the "set" of postulants who entered six months before. I was not merely an add-on to the group, my directress had told me; they had saved me a place. My arrival completed the set, and with members aged twenty, twenty-one, twenty-seven, twenty-eight, and sixty, it was an extraordinary set indeed.

Traditionally, formation was never a popular segment of religious life, and I carried on the tradition. I struggled in those beginning years, not because they were devoid of value, but because sometimes the value was lost in the maze of restrictions. I came to the community at age twenty-eight, with a well-developed spirituality, fashioned by study and strengthened by storm, and I resisted and resented the notion that I needed to be "formed." And while all who associated with us recognized that we were not the seventeen-year-olds of a past era, few knew how to translate that reality into practice.

In retrospect, my adjustment was fairly smooth. The frustration born of rules and rigidity paled in comparison to the joy I experienced in finally being "at home." The nuns of my youth and adolescence became my sisters. Living among them, I was keenly aware of being surrounded by my personal history, while being overwhelmed at the privilege to be part of their present and future. I had no doubt that I was where I belonged. On August 3, 1986, I professed final vows as an Ursuline of Cleveland, making a forever gift of myself to God in this company of Saint Angela Merici.

Whatever disappointment I experienced in the early years came from the Sisters' reticence in talking about religion or faith. To their credit, they taught with zeal and truly lived a deep and vibrant faith, but discussing it among themselves was another story. They were products of training that had fostered a private prayer life in quiet individual pursuit of the way of perfection. By contrast, I came from an experience of Church that encouraged group prayer, lively dialogue, and personal witness. Throughout the years many of the Sisters have taught me the value of reflection; I hope I have enriched them as well by sharing my story and by encouraging them to do the same.

My ministry as an Ursuline Sister has taken many shapes and forms. I have served as a parish pastoral minister, as a nurse's aide in the community infirmary, as a college campus minister, and as a communications specialist in development and public relations. While I like to think I've been "dynamically adaptable to the needs of the times," as Saint Angela directed in her writings, it's probably more accurate to say that I enjoy variety and welcome change. In reality, it's a combination of those truths, and in that can be found the heart of ministry for me. What I am able to do, I will gladly do; wherever I serve, I will serve faithfully.

I have been awed and enriched by persons and experiences in each place I have served: by the young college student, unmarried and pregnant, seeking from me the wisdom of the Church and the compassion of Jesus; by the gnarled old woman I visited on parish Communion calls, whose greatest joy was the Eucharist; and by the eighty-nine-year-old Sister crying softly for her mother. Each and every one has changed me.

My life in the Ursuline congregation has been free of the serious unrest and turmoil that marked the community in the sixties and seventies. Our Chapter deliberations finally laid to rest the discussions of what we wear and how we pray, so that together we can consider the more pressing issues of who we are as women, as religious, as members of the Church—and what we are called to do for love of God and God's people.

Who is Angela Merici to me in all of this? I must confess, if I had pondered this question even a year ago, my answer would have been far different than it is today. As a novice I studied her writings and recited the Angela prayers others had composed. While I regarded this remarkable woman with genuine respect and admiration, I couldn't say that I knew her personally or felt a strong spirit bond with her. She was simply the historic starting point of the community with whom I dared to cast my lot.

I see now that the picture of Angela I hold in my mind's eye is a composite representation of all the Ursuline Sisters I have known here and beyond Cleveland's boundaries; those I have loved and respected, and those I have found difficult to like. Angela has been part of my journey from the very beginning, incarnated and enfleshed for me through all of the Ursuline Sisters who taught me, formed me, encouraged me, and finally welcomed me into their company. They have brought Angela to life for me. They have challenged me to accept the best and the worst life has to offer, and to trust that living as Angela encouraged, "bound one to the other by the bond of charity, respecting ... helping...bearing with each other in Christ," we can make our way through the difficulties of life to the sweet love that is its very center.

My life as an Ursuline has not been especially significant or noteworthy, but it is the life to which I have been called, through which I am strengthened, and by which I hope to serve God's people. Truly, I believe that the real story of my Ursuline life is the journey I traveled to begin it. That pilgrimage, lined with disappointing twists and gut-wrenching turns—and resplendent with sacred people and grace-filled moments—led me to a marvelous place and a journey that remains forever beginning.

Woman, Latin American, and Ursuline on the Way

ADRIANA MENDEZ-PENATE, OSU

The darkness is not dark to you;
the night is as bright as the day....
You knit me together in my mother's womb.
I praise you, for I am fearfully and wonderfully made.
—PSALM 139:12,13,14

It was a lifetime ago. I felt alone. I was very sad. Like the Little Prince, I went to the beach every day and watched the sun set, wondering what would happen. Sometimes I wondered if I would ever see that same sun again. I had never really thought about the possibility of leaving Cuba, my parents, and everything dear to me to become an Ursuline for the sake of Jesus Christ. But there I was, almost ready to leave everything—not for Jesus, but on account of Fidel Castro.

I didn't know what to think or do; it was a time of darkness for me. I was losing the Way. Schools were closed. The Ursulines had left. I couldn't study anymore. The Catholic university was taken over by Castro. My parents were worried because they felt I was too outspoken and could easily get into trouble. Several of my friends had already been put in jail for that very reason: they were Catholics so they had to be against Castro because he was a Communist.

At the time I wasn't old enough to understand the difference and to make my own decisions. When my aunts, uncles, and cousins started leaving for the United States, my parents insisted that I leave, too, with my recently married sister who was going to New York City with her husband. My father had received an invitation to go to Mérida, Yucatán, Mexico, for a medical conference, so my parents would try to leave the country later. But they wanted me to leave immediately.

I knew I wanted to be a real Catholic, and I thought that Communism was very bad. I thought that faith and political commitment were as incompatible as oil and water. I felt I had to choose between Christ and Cuba. I chose to leave my beloved Cuba.

I didn't know where I was going or where Jesus was leading me, but I knew I had to leave. I was eighteen and a half when I left Havana—my small planet, my Mother Earth—on July 6, 1961. I felt uprooted. I was on the Way.

I have the feeling that the Gardener never planted me again. Every now and then I feel like Philip in the Acts of the Apostles; the Voice calls, "Go toward the south to the road that goes down from Jerusalem" (8:26). At other times I feel like a child; darkness and sudden sadness take hold of me and I ask, "Are you running with me, Jesus?" Often, now as before, I don't know where I'm going; I only know I am on the Way. Occasionally, the Spirit snatches me away, and I experience the privilege of walking toward the Sun, searching for New Light, leading a new Life. This search for Light and real Life have kept me alive, praying, learning, realizing, understanding, intuiting, becoming, struggling for justice, working in the basic ecclesial communities, and falling in love with Jesus through the gospels and the Scriptures.

I was eighteen when I was about to leave Cuba in 1961. Now, in my mid fifties, I realize that all along I have had a growing awareness of myself, first as a Latin American (Cuban-Mexican), then as an Ursuline, and last—surprisingly—as a woman. Today, this trinity is so tightly braided, so closely knit, that it is all that I am.

Actually, I wasn't aware of this trinity until very recently. It is only now, in the autumn of my life, that I feel God doing as my mother used to do. When I was a little girl, my mother would wash my long dark hair and leave it loose to dry. I would go out on the balcony, in the sun, and play "the lion and the tamer" with my sister, Martha—I was the lion, of course. When my hair dried, it was always tangled, so my mother would comb and braid it for me. This was a routine Saturday morning ritual. In the same way, the Lord has been patiently combing and braiding the strands of my life in his own time and in his own way.

This insight moved me strongly on my thirty-day retreat during my renewal period in Rome. I asked myself what it meant for me to be a woman and an Ursuline in Latin America. I didn't care whether I was at the head, heart, or toe of the world; I was searching for "all that I am." I told myself that I had only one life to live and that it was essential for me to make myself one and to integrate my history and my present so that I could be a real *Latin American Ursuline woman.*

Come with me. Let us take each other by the hand. As I tell you my story, perhaps we can birth each other. Perhaps you will help me and I will help you, and together we will find the loving and eternal Braider of our lives, the true Light, and true Way.

My name is Adriana. During my childhood, I learned that this name came from *ad-oriens* and meant "rising sun." When I learned this I believed that my call was to walk in the light, to give light. In Spanish, when a woman gives birth to a child we say "*Dio a luz*" (She gave light). I feel I have the feminine call to give birth and light to those I find on my Way.

In the braiding of my life, everything started in a simple way, but all three strands have been present since the beginning. Angela Merici, the foundress of the Ursulines, has been my friend for as long as I can remember. I met her when I met Jesus and Mary, but studied her extensively during tertianship. As I read her life and writings, along with the gospels, I became aware of the fact that my spirituality—everything I said, prayed, or did to live the "twofold love" and to have "Jesus known, loved, and adored by all nations" as a woman religious—had been no different from what any male religious would think or do.

Since my school days I had identified with Saint Peter; it never occurred to me that maleness or femaleness made a difference in the following of Jesus. During tertianship, however, things started changing inside me. I became more aware of being a woman, of having a woman foundress. I discovered that Angela related to Jesus in a very different way from Peter, Paul, Ignatius, Francis, or other male saints.

It struck me that a stone, a flower, or a fruit shows forth in its unique way, something of the Artist who created it. I asked myself: *What is it that I have as a woman that shows the hand of my Maker?* I realized that as a "hand-made" of the Lord, from head to toe, I should give glory as a woman to the Artist who did such a good job.

I am delighted to have had a woman foundress. I believe that Angela, in many ways, is leading the Way. To know Angela and her femininity in the fifteenth century is a fountain of joy and hope for me. Even with my twentieth-century Latin American mentality, I can easily identify with Angela in her feminine approach to motherhood, to her life-giving spirit, to her gifts of reconciliation, love, and friendship, to the way she related to people. Her love for Jesus impelled me to study about women in the Bible—especially in the gospels—about our relationship with Jesus, our only treasure, and about his liberating message to us as women.

I have written articles and books in which I have tried to read the gospels from a woman's point of view, emphasizing "where" or "how" we are situated in our reality. I have come to understand that if women are different from men and other creatures, then women must find their own unique way of "directing everything towards the praise and the glory of his Majesty and the good of souls" (Angela's Prologue to the Counsels).

Discovering myself as a woman living in Mexico has also made me realize how close I am to nature. Our ancestors gave "God power" to the land and made the earth their God-mother (goddess). For thousands of years, they called their land *Pachamama* or *Tonantzin*, which means "Mother Earth." Although Christianity does not have the concept of a mother goddess, somewhere in the heart of the Mexican people, the extraordinary love for Our Lady of Guadalupe is a cry for justice and equality. María de Guadalupe, as in the *Magnificat*, sides with the poor and shows a different image of the loving God.

Like Mary and Angela, like the moon, like Mother Earth and her seasons, I—as a woman—live in a continuous cycle and in a spiraling, growing, and moving paschal mystery, always in the middle of a step, always on the Way, always coming or going every twenty-eight days in a creating or dying process of life, giving birth, giving light. I have to smile when I think that the most stable thing we, as women, have is our constant cycle.

I introduced myself as a Latin American. More specifically, I am a Cuban-Mexican. I am a Cuban, born of Cuban parents in 1943, in Havana, Cuba, tropical island of sun and sea. I am a Mexican-made nun, "born" in 1963, in Puebla, of the Mexican Province of the Roman Union of Saint Ursula. My very Cuban family was quite small, by Cuban standards, especially on my mother's side. My mother's name is Adriana Herrera Pedroche. Her parents left Spain on their wedding day, and that was the last time my grandmother saw her own family. My grandfather died of the flu when my mother's older sister was ten years old; my mother was six and the youngest was four. Because the executor stole my grandfather's pharmacy, my mother was forced to start working at the age of fourteen—an experience that made her distrustful of people the rest of her life.

My dad, Ricardo Méndez-Peñate Rodríguez, was born July 7, 1907 (07/07/07), in Las Villas on a tobacco plantation. He was the eldest of five brothers. The family had been in Cuba for many generations, during which time several of my dad's uncles had become involved in politics. It was almost impossible to live in Cuba without being in some way affected by the political situation. For example, my mom and dad met in Havana in 1928, when they were sixteen and twenty-one, but they didn't marry until December 20, 1939: eleven years later. Because of the political situation, my father's medical studies had been interrupted, so they had to delay the marriage.

I have one sister, Martha, who is a year and ten months older than I and lives in Puerto Rico with her husband, Santiago. They have two married daughters, a thirteen-year-old son, and three grandsons.

Like many Latin American women, I grew up feeling I wasn't worth as much as a man because I was female. In fact, since Martha was a girl, my parents expected me to be a boy. I was to be named Ricardo, after my father. Instead, I arrived—so my father named me after my two grandmothers. Florinda, my dad's mother, and Adriana, my mother's mother. Actually, my whole first name is Adriana Flora. This made me "Adrianita, la chiquita" (little little Adriana) because I was the third.

Since my dad was the only man in our family of four, my mom, a real Latin American wife and mother, educated my sister and me. We knew that my dad was the king of the house and of our world; when he appeared on the scene and my sister and I were fighting or arguing, it was as if a bell rang and each boxer would return to her respective corner. My mother seemed to totally forget herself. Dad, Martha, and I filled her life. She worried especially about my father's needs. I remember the many times—even after I became a nun—when I would kiss her, and she would say, "Go kiss your father." She was always alert for ways in which the three of us women could make my dad happy—and I think we succeeded until he died, the day after their fifty-first wedding anniversary. Needless to say, it took me quite a while to realize that being male is not inherently "better," and that we are all equals.

I also grew up with a specific set of ideas concerning pain. As long as I can remember, Dad fought suffering and illness with all his heart. Perhaps this partially accounts for why he became an anesthesiologist; Dad couldn't stand to see anyone suffer. When we were ill, he would buy us a toy every day. When I was thirteen, my sister and I were in a car accident, and several pieces of the windshield pierced my face. I was taken to the clinic where my dad was in an operating room with a patient. I kept asking for him, and until he came and assured me that I would be all right, I would not let anyone touch me. He finally "put me to sleep," and I was operated on. Even though this seems an unimportant incident, the memory has stayed with me.

My tertian directress once asked me, "Adriana, why are you always trying to anesthetize yourself?" I couldn't answer that question in 1979; today I can. The question of suffering and its meaning in our lives has always been important to me. In a booklet I wrote on the Gospel of Mark, I maintain that the Father didn't want the suffering or death of his Son. Rather, God used his power to bring good out of the evil that we had done. For me, suffering is not a value; it is just the way to Resurrection and Life, the path or first step of the paschal mystery. I realize that we must go through the pains of labor if we are to see the new Life and its fruit (John 16:21). I believe that the Cross isn't a gift from God; Light and Life cannot give darkness or death even if they wanted to. For years I have heard religious people say to battered women that theirs is the cross God wants them to carry. Surely God is not like Huitzilopochtli, the god of war, who was fed with the hearts of the victims.

But all these thoughts came much later. As a child I lived the normal Cuban childhood of a middle-class family. We roller skated and even ice skated, and I had a motor bike and a beautiful German Shepherd: Prince.

As an extrovert, I was always ready to play; I found cooking and sewing lessons far less interesting. Two happy summers were spent in a camp where I was named chief of the Mohawks. Of course, I studied too, but only enough to get by. Like many girls, I kept a diary; mine was addressed to my guardian angel whom I named Carioca.

I learned to relate with God and others through my relationship with my parents. I grew close to them and felt proud when someone said I looked like my dad. Often, when he finished his work at the hospital, Dad would take me to the beach and we would spend several hours in our motor boat or swimming. Mom and Martha seldom joined us because they were fair-skinned; they couldn't remain in the sun for long periods of time.

I always knew when my father was annoyed; he grew silent. As a child, I could not bear this and would do anything in the world to get him to talk to me again. Later in life, I discovered that this was one of my patterns. If a friend stopped talking to me, I would experience the same feeling I had as a child. In a way I have had this same experience in prayer. Fortunately, God is never completely silent. The whole of creation speaks to me of his love for me. Just taking a deep breath every now and then reminds me that God is with me, praying, working, running, sitting—with me and in me, and I in him.

In many little ways the divine Braider got an early start weaving the strands of my life together. My hunger and thirst for justice were nursed by the Lord since my early days. When I played with other children, I made sure everything was kept "fair." Even now, I prefer to toss a coin and let "luck" decide when "a better chance" is at risk. My commitment to the cause of justice, to Catholic Action, and later on to basic ecclesial communities and liberation theology took root in my childhood experiences.

As time goes by, I am increasingly aware of the lack of equality between First World and Third World countries. For example, the religious, social, cultural, political, and economic conditions of our Latin American countries have been deplorable throughout history. Before and after the Second Vatican Council, all the bishops' conferences—from Río de Janeiro (1956), Medellín (1968), through Puebla (1979) and Santo Domingo (1992)—have denounced the unjust conditions of our society. The military governments, the dictatorships, the corruption, the hunger and misery of the people, have forced millions of Latin Americans to live in extreme poverty; many have been led to martyrdom as a result of their speaking out on justice issues. Thus, our environment has imbued us with the drive for justice and the desire for peace, just as if it were our mother's milk.

My meeting with the Ursulines was another gift of the divine Braider. We were "Catholic" but my parents didn't practice much. From 1948 until 1960, Martha and I studied in the two Ursuline schools of Havana, where my parents sent us to learn English. The Ursulines of the Roman Union had two schools in Cuba: Merici Academy and Ursulinas de Miramar. From preprimary through seventh grade, I attended Merici Academy, an English-speaking school founded by Sisters of the Central Province. For my secondary level education, I went to Ursulinas de Miramar, a Spanish school run by Cuban Sisters. From the Ursuline Sisters, I learned about the Lord—and I learned English.

My vocation as an Ursuline took root in 1949, when I was six years old. My mom and dad were invited to South America, and Martha and I were sent to the Ursuline boarding school for six months. I loved to listen to the Sisters chant the Office of Our Lady, or hear them laugh at recreation time. When I returned home I made a prayer corner for myself, filled my night table with saints, and kept a collection of novenas in my dresser drawer; I said my prayers on a bathroom rug and rubber kneeler. Catechism was my favorite subject. I memorized one hundred questions on Saint Angela for a contest we had. I loved to work for the missions and saved twenty dollars in my own piggy bank to help my class accumulate the biggest donation.

On the first Friday of each month, I helped prepare the altar for Mass in the auditorium and felt honored to take the candle to accompany the Blessed Sacrament back to chapel when Mass was over. Mother Berchmans Forgey was my third-grade teacher and she prepared me for first Holy Communion and confirmation in 1950. When I grew older I got a Spanish-Latin daily missal to help me better follow the Mass, and in Catholic Action I was given a New Testament to learn the method of "see, think, and act," which I have followed ever since.

After I made my first Holy Communion, I started questioning my parents; I asked them to take us to Mass. They wanted to be consistent with what they had chosen for us, so they made every effort to take us each Sunday. I had my first "paschal experience" at the age of thirteen, during my first three-day retreat. On the second day of the retreat, a Jesuit priest gave us a talk on Our Lady, on her *fiat* and her readiness to love and be loved by the Word. I was deeply touched by what Father said, and consider that my "first conversion." I went to confession, but cried so hard that I could manage to say only a few things to receive absolution. Later that day I pounded the wall with my fist and literally told the devil that I didn't want anything to do with him anymore.

Today I believe this experience changed something inside of me, leaving a strong mark on my life. I believe I received a genuine actual grace that has lasted forever. It was an experience of new Life, of being raised from the dead just as Jairus' daughter was. Jesus took me by the hand and brought me close to him. Even today, when the child in me dies, I go near Jesus, "touch the edge of his cloak" or let him take hold of my hand, and listen to him whisper to my heart, "Child, get up" (see Luke 8:40–56).

Each year the Ursuine Sisters invited me to a retreat. Although I could feel the Lord calling me during those days, as soon as the retreat ended, I tried to forget the experience and return to my ordinary life, with the exception of daily Mass and Holy Communion, which became a great need that has lasted through the years. I joined the Infant Jesus Sodality, was a Child of Mary, and was very involved in Catholic Action—all this along with a vigorous social life as well. I had a boyfriend who studied in the United States. When he came home on vacations, I gave him a hard time by making him go to Mass and Holy Communion with me. Some of his Protestant friends confused him about the Church and Our Lady, so I bought and studied booklets on how to answer questions a Protestant might raise about the Catholic faith. Instead of sending love letters to my boyfriend, I sent him "theological epistles."

As I grew out of childhood, I became aware of other realities besides family, school, beach, parties, and friends. There was our Cuban history—a human drama that changed the lives of all Cubans. Whether we remained in the country or not, our personal stories were intricately braided into that history.

Not only Cuba, but Mexico and most Latin American countries have experienced horrible turmoil throughout their respective histories. Not one of our countries has known peace or democracy in the past five hundred years. Discovered on October 27, 1492, Cuba was the first area to be colonized but unfortunately, the last place to get its "independence." Finally, in 1895, José Martí started the Independence War.

When Spain lost the war of 1898 to the United States, it surrendered Cuba. In 1902 we had our first president, but when my father was born in 1907, American forces once again occupied Cuba. In 1909 there was a second Republic, followed by several revolts and dictatorships. Through it all, and into the current political situation, the United States kept a military presence at Guantanamo Base.

In 1933 there was a revolt of the Army, and Fulgencio Batista came to power. With the support of the United States, Batista—a corrupt and brutal dictator—governed for seventeen of the twenty-five years between 1934 and 1959. This period spanned my parents' youth, marriage, and my birth and childhood.

I started raising questions about justice issues, poverty, Communism, capitalism, and the following of Christ in my religion class. At the time, Sister Lorraine Pomerleau—my teacher and the school directress—listened to me and accompanied me in my search.

By the 1950s the political situation in Cuba had become especially difficult. Under Batista's dictatorship, people lived in uncertainty. Many were imprisoned and tortured; others disappeared. Almost everyone was in favor of a revolution.

On July 26, 1953, Fidel Castro and a group of men attacked the Cuartel Moncada in Santiago de Cuba. The attack was unsuccessful, and Castro was imprisoned until 1955, at which time he left for Mexico. There he initiated the 26th of July Movement and in December 1956 returned to Cuba. Again the revolt was unsuccessful. Everyone was killed, except Castro and eleven others who hid themselves in the Sierra Maestra, the mountains in Santiago de Cuba. That's when the guerrilla war started. The government repression became even stronger, and the populace grew to hate Batista even more.

On January 1, 1959, Batista fled the country, and on January 8—my sixteenth birthday—Castro triumphantly entered Havana. I was in my fourth year of preuniversity studies in Ursulinas de Miramar.

Most Cubans were happy with Castro. He talked for hours on television, and we were convinced that his revolution was "as Cuban as the palm of his hand." But by November of that year, our new political leader was talking about Communism and expressing clear opposition to Catholicism.

I graduated in June 1960 and enrolled that fall in the only Catholic university we had—Santo Tomás de Villanueva—where I completed one semester in psychology. With the direction of Father Botey, we started a community of students who prayed, sang, fasted, and studied together.

In January 1961, when I was in my second semester at the university, the United States ended diplomatic relations with Cuba. At this time, the North American Ursuline Sisters left Cuba and some Cuban Sisters who lived in the States returned to keep the work going in the two schools.

Martha had already left Cuba. She married Santiago Segurola on December 11, 1960, and a week later left for New York. There, Sister Marie McCullogh, who had taught in Cuba, helped them find jobs and later got a visa for me to enter the United States.

In April 1961, during Kennedy's administration, a group of Cubans unsuccessfully invaded the Bay of Pigs and were subsequently imprisoned. At that time, Castro took over the Catholic schools and the university. Many people had already started to leave the country. The soldiers were everywhere. They took over the houses of the *gusanos* (worms): those who left Cuba. Everyone was afraid to talk; we didn't know who could be trusted, who would denounce us.

And here I am, back at the beginning, where I started with all that I am. On July 6, 1961, I arrived in New York City and lived with Martha and Santiago, who were expecting their first baby. With my refugee status and my grasp of the English language, I was able to get a job as a file clerk in Bankers Trust Company in Wall Street. I studied at Saint John's University for a semester, continuing my daily routine of going to Mass. When I didn't have classes, I worked overtime. On Saturday nights I tried to have a good time by meeting my Cuban friends to chat and dance, but I wasn't happy. Somehow, I felt cheated. I had fled Cuba, running away from Communism, and ended up on a control desk of the pension division department that dealt with stocks and bonds of transnational companies making lots and lots of money in seconds. I learned much about being a refugee, about capitalism, about receiving less salary just because I was a refugee, about what a consumer society was, and about the fever of earning as much money as possible in as short a time as possible. I felt that capitalism was not the answer either. My Cuban sun wasn't there with me, and again I was impelled to search for the Light.

On Holy Thursday 1962, I finally accepted my Ursuline vocation. I had kept in close contact with the Ursulines who had been in Cuba, and I asked them to receive me as a postulant in Puebla, Mexico, for the Latin American Province. For me, it was a choice between getting married or being a Latin American Ursuline.

In the meantime, my parents relocated to Mérida, Yucatán, in Mexico, where my dad found work at the Social Security hospital. When they suggested I join them and study at the Jesuit university in Mexico, I accepted. I wanted everything back so I could give it up again, but this time, it would be for Jesus Christ.

When I told my parents I wanted to become a nun, we all cried; it wasn't easy for any of us. My parents had been willing to lose everything in Cuba so they wouldn't have to lose us—and there I was, becoming a nun at a time when, according to Ursuline rules, I would never be allowed to go home again. As it is, I went home for the first time seven years later, when my parents celebrated their thirtieth wedding anniversary.

On February 5, 1963, just at the beginning of the Second Vatican Council, two Mexican women and I entered as postulants. Mother María Balandra, now in heaven, was our novice mistress. My training involved very little of the old monastic lifestyle since Vatican II changes were coming so quickly. I made solemn vows in 1980, lived through the time of transition and experimentation, and survived to enjoy the time of renewal that finally came after that.

In a way, my novitiate was another paschal experience for me. My faith was growing; I was happy with prayer and community life—and with Jesus; I could accept anything and everything for him. Yet I felt completely "disconnected from the world" that I thought I had to know and love in order to help. I felt set back in my efforts to integrate my faith and my political commitment.

I spent my five year juniorate between Mexico City and Puebla. I studied to be a primary teacher and a catechist, and studied theology for two semesters at the Jesuit university. I also taught. But my love was the missions. For me, going on mission was an opportunity to work closely with the poor in rural areas where they seldom heard the Word of God. I became involved with groups that prepared Holy Week missions, in which several seminarians, a priest, a Sister, and young boys and girls would visit people in their homes and invite them to church and to liturgies. But it wasn't enough; I wanted full-time mission work.

The 1968 Bishop's Conference of Medellín opened the doors of Vatican II to Latin America. At last we were being awakened to the cry of the Latin American people for justice and peace and the teaching of dogma. In 1970, while the basic ecclesial communities were developing in several countries, I was teaching second-graders and preparing to celebrate final vows on August 6, the feast of the Transfiguration.

At this time a group of Ursulines asked permission to develop an experimental community in Mexico City. With our former provincial serving as our superior, we moved out of the big convent, rented a little house nearby, and continued to work at the Ursuline school. For several years we continued our experimentation with prayer, community, and group sharing.

During Holy Week 1971, a further opportunity was offered me: I was invited to go with a group of former classmates to a mission in Guanajuato. The group was guided by a Jesuit seminarian, Javier Saravia, an economist interested in justice issues and the development of the people. The following year he planned a month's mission to celebrate his ordination. This time a young man, two peasants, a Sister of Saint Jospeh, and I accompanied him. Within the month we visited eleven communities, offering them the Word of God incarnated in their reality. In helping the people better understand their situations and problems, I myself began to understand more fully.

In 1973 we were invited to join a new type of mixed communities, comprising five Jesuits, a laywoman, three Sisters of Charity, and three Ursulines. We set up our community in a rural area of Tabasco, a southern state bordering the Gulf of Mexico, a place resembling my homeland. We named the community ERIT: Equipo Rural Inter-religioso en Tabasco. At last I had the opportunity of living in a full-time mission.

The parish was a difficult one, consisting mostly of the Chontales Indians, very poor and uneducated people. The Sisters lived in a small round stick house with a thatched roof. We called it "the Sun." It was made more colorful by a profusion of floods, heat, rats, and mosquitoes. A whole year had gone by. During that year we had to leave our original parish and begin in another because of Church difficulties.

I went to ERIT when I was thirty years old, and left eleven years later. I consider that experience one of the greatest gifts the Lord has given me. In spite of storms and cloudy days, I felt "my Cuban sun alive and bright." I grew to understand that the only way to bring the kingdom of God into our midst is by working for justice at the economic level; by working for peace at the political level; and by working for truth and love at the social, religious, and cultural levels. If we want to live the "twofold" love of God and neighbor, we have to let Jesus be known, and we have to work in consciousness-raising and evangelization. Angela Merici, in her Fourth Counsel, insists that we be well aware of "the needs of our Sisters, both spiritual and temporal."

Throughout that experience, I learned to live much closer to the people. We had eighty-six communities, or *rancherías* to attend; each one with a church of its own. We started the basic ecclesial communities, organized cooperative groups that had stores, sold bananas, and grew chickens. We studied our reality and the Bible; we celebrated our faith. We made weekly themes for the *animators* (facilitators) of the communities. I learned to write the themes and became involved in reading the Bible, searching for simple ways, like parables, group dynamics, and exercises, to convey Jesus' message. In addition to this work, Father Javier has written several books on the Bible and has taught many courses. I have had the grace and privilege of editing most of his work and teaching courses with him.

Each congregation had its little stick house to sleep in. Work, meetings, prayer, Eucharist, meals, cars, money: all these were shared in common. We used the Latin American method of "see, think, act": a method that involved putting God's Word into practice in our daily lives. A strong friendship and fraternal relation helped us overcome the difficulties of daily living and guided us in our efforts to embrace our apostolate. We took the time each week to plan and evaluate, always in an attempt to find better ways of doing things.

In 1984, I left ERIT for Puebla to be the directress of the postulants. I arrived on March 5. Twenty days later, on the feast of the Annunciation, I was asked by our superior general to accept the responsibilities of provincial of Mexico. I accepted and, beginning July 15, served 2 three-year terms.

I lived many experiences throughout this time: meetings in Rome, research on Angela, my growing prayer life, and the fact that I was working in the internal affairs of my community. I dealt with the closing of houses, the sickness and death of eight Sisters, the growing needs of the older Sisters, the new life of the young postulants and novices, the need for community leadership in the province and in formation, the lack of money.

By 1988 the personnel in ERIT had completely changed, and the day came when we were asked to leave because we didn't have the personnel to serve. This was one of the most difficult moments of my life. It was like killing my son, Isaac. My sacrifice was short-lived however. Within a short time, the bishop insisted that we return to the diocese. In October 1990, we went to another parish in Tabasco.

Presently, I belong to a group of "Popular Biblists." We study the Bible and create materials that help put the Word of God in the hands and the hearts of all the people. We meet once a year as a group, and strive to provide personal and spiritual support to one another at all times. In 1988, I wrote a book on women and the Gospel of Luke. I often teach three-day courses, sharing with my women companions, trying to help them read the Bible from their hearts and their "feminine side."

I served my last year as provincial in 1990. My term ended in August, right after my silver jubilee. From 1990 to the celebration of my fiftieth birthday—a half a century—I lived through many significant paschal experiences. They were years of loss. My dear Braider had decided, I guess, to make me realize that *Solo Dios basta* (Only God is enough) and that he is my only "sun."

In February 1990, I went to Mérida with my parents. I stayed with my dad for three days while my mother went to Houston for her medical check-up. When I accompanied him to the doctor to get sleeping pills, he was admitted to the hospital for the night; no one knew that he had suffered a silent heart attack and needed complete bed rest.

In the meantime, I began to experience frequent hemorrhages, and subsequently found out that I needed a hysterectomy. I returned to Mérida from Puebla on April 3 for the operation, and my dad's doctor gave him permission to be there with me. Because of the tension in my life at the time, I developed high blood pressure and have been on medication ever since. That same year, Dad died—the day after he and Mom celebrated their fifty-first wedding anniversary. Fortunately, Martha and I were both there. God, in his loving providence, took Dad home in seconds, in the way that he had asked the Lord. The Lord was with him as my dad was with me.

In closing, I share one meaningful moment of my recent past. On January 8, 1993, I celebrated half a century in this world. I invited my small community and some friends to share the day with me, among them, Father Javier who celebrated the Eucharist. Again, I was at the beach, like I was so many years ago as a young girl—but this time, I was not alone. In the evening, as we walked along the shore toward the sun, waiting for it to set, I was happy. The sunset was beautiful. Yet it wasn't enough; I seemed to need more. So we waited for the moon to birth, the first full moon of the year.

My fiftieth birthday made a difference in my life. I found myself again snatched by the Spirit, but that time, I was giving birth to moons and Earth. Enough of brilliance! Enough of sun!

For my birthday, a young friend of mine gave me a poem, in Spanish. It captures part of my story that day—and today. The author's pen name is Isabel Guerrero (Elizabeth Warrior).

BIRTHS

I

I'm giving birth to autumns in my soul.
Love and nostalgia are being born from me.
Sunsets spring forth in me.
and I fill myself of autumn dreams.

I dress myself in dim clarity.
Enough of brilliance!
Enough of suns!
Moons are being born in my body.
Cosmic Earth springs out of me.

II

I am birthing soon towards life.
Life is springing out in the midst of autumn.
EARTH lulls me in her beat
and Earth I'm giving birth,
new worlds.

New worlds, and new realities
are springing out from me.
I'm birthing out free, towards mystery.
Hatred dies in me.
I give death to injustice
and I give birth to brethren among the people.

III

I give life and I ask for life.
I exchange blood for sap.
I die with your death,
Sister Earth,
and the world dies in me from within.

I give sudden death to poverty
and abundance springs out from me among
    all people.
Autumn shouts: Enough of selfishness;
let us kill Violence,
let us bury all deaths,
let us bury miseries!
Let us procreate life, companions!

I V

I want to be born again
from the womb of my people.
I want to sprout from
 the dark and peasant skin.
I want to enter the fraternal and prophetic
womb of the historical hope of workers.

I want to be born a thousand times
to give new life.

Let the people and their courage
fecundate me
so that I can give birth to new beings,
new life, new heavens and new earths.

In response to that gift, I wrote a poem for my friend:

For Elizabeth Warrior,
who being in full spring
intuits the autumn of my life.
    "For a time, and times, and half a time."
           REVELATION 12:14

There is time to give and time to receive;
time to read and time to write;
time to speak and time to hear;
time to suffer and die;
time to enjoy and live.

I am in Paschal time,
in the middle of a time,
time of passing, time of interval;
one foot on high, another on Earth.
I'm on my Way, half way!

You, Friend, die in full spring,
I die in the autumn of my life.
I die, live and pass every day
with the Moon, the Earth and the tides.

Keep on writing, Elizabeth,
your sterility is gone.
"Your opprobrium and humiliation
among men are over..." (Luke 4:25)
It is time to bear and give fruit...

So the word became flesh,
*and was mad*e letter, psalm, *and* woman.

Yes, I have found that it isn't too late. Now is the time to pray and write in *woman's* tone. I want to birth the earth. For many centuries, with a few exceptions (such as the Counsels and Legacies of Angela Merici, and some other writings), our brothers have written about us women, for us women, and always from their point of view. That is why I don't want to write as we "normally do" in an impersonal way or in third person. I want to keep on writing as a *woman*, who is *Latin American* and *Ursuline*, daughter of Angela Merici. I wish that my flesh, blood, and life may become *letter*, *word*, and *Scripture*.

I wanted to share this poem because I believe it shows forth the three strands of the braid of my life, as far as they are today. Perhaps I'm half-way or, maybe, toward the end of the braid; it doesn't matter. The important thing is that I'm here, with all that I am. The poem throws a light on yesterday and makes me realize the loving presence of the divine Braider, in whom I live and move. In him I exist. God is my Father, my Mother, my Everyone.

I know that my divine Braider hasn't finished combing my life. I know that I can be idealistic, that I tend to make "idols" of circumstances, people, places, or friends, especially when I undervalue or underestimate myself. These insights have made me react in a new way. I can't stand violence. I wholeheartedly want to put to death and bury all injustice; I want to liberate the woman in me; I want all women and men to be free and born again.

I believe that after my fiftieth birthday, Jesus again touched me and woke me up. My mother spent Lent with me in Tabasco and accompanied me to all the *rancherías*. There was nothing to tell us apart. We laughed; we cried; we shared many of the secrets of our hearts. With a word, with a question, we shared—and what was there, hidden and buried, soon came to light. We prayed together until the first full moon of spring:

> *We are reborn again, we have gone back*
> *to our origin*
> *to the wombs of our mothers; there where*
> *"we feel embraced behind and before us,*
> *there where our inmost being was formed*
> *and knitted..."*

"I give you thanks, Mother, for all the wonders…
wonderful are your works, and my soul really
     knows it…"

My frame was not unknown to you,
when I was made in the secret,
when I was fashioned in the depth of the
earth (Psalm 139:3, 13, 16).

Women, why do you weep?
the opprobrium among men is gone…

Be not afraid, you have found grace before God.

Elizabeth and I are fruitful women.
We are birthing LIFE.
We have been given the two wings of the
     gigantic eagle,
so that we can fly to our place in the desert,
where far from the serpent we will be taken care of
for a time, for two and a half times
     more (Revelation 12:14).

Jesus keeps touching me and teaching me both new lessons
and old. I do not have to run away from suffering; he wants
me to understand that he is my only treasure. In the autumn
of my life, when I am not youthful Mary, but more like older
Elizabeth or Angela, I realize that *"Rising Sun and Bright-*
ness" have become *"Full Moon and Dim Clarity."* Full Moon is
now close, very close to Mother Earth. Full Moon realizes
that she shines and bears fruit, not with her own light and
life but with the Light and Life that has been given to her.
She and Mother Earth know that suffering is necessary (Luke

24:7,26,46). They know themselves as mothers, having one and the same spirituality of *fecundity*, giving life and light in a simple way, opening themselves to receive and transform every gift into new Life.

There are many ways in which I can give birth as an Ursuline here and now in Latin America. In the last twenty years we have had more martyrs than in the first three centuries of the Church. Yesterday it was Ursula and her companions, later, the martyrs of Valenciennes and Orange. Today it is Bishop Romero, Sister Dorothy Kazel, and the Jesuits and laywomen in El Salvador and in other countries. They not only led the Way, but have gone all the Way; they were in love and are where Love took them. It seems to me that Love goes that far. One wants to be in the Presence of the Loved One, do things for him, and become one with him wherever he may lead. Our martyrs have suffered and shed their blood to give birth to New People. I don't have to anesthetize myself—in fact, I don't want to anesthetize myself. I want to let the Spirit snatch me over and over again.

Today I understand much better why Angela gave us Ursula and her companions as patronesses, and why she refers continually to the Passion of Jesus. She is sorry for "not having shed a drop of her blood for Jesus." Her heart bleeds and breaks. She would willingly "shed her blood if it would be sufficient to cure the blindness of those that do not want to share his Passion."

There is a great deal of pain among our people, within families, within our communities, within the political parties, among nations, in all spheres of life. I feel the call to make the spirit of Angela present in our midst through our compassionate love and the gift of reconciliation that is our heritage.

Angela is the true mother of our company; she is "always in our midst," with Jesus, "the one who loves us all," the true Son of Mary, who compared himself to a mother hen that "gathers her brood under her wings" (Luke 13:34). I believe that Jesus, he who loves us, is alive and living in me. I feel "chosen to be the true and chaste bride of the Son of God... what a new and marvelous dignity" (Prologue of the Rule).

As a Latin American Ursuline woman, I realize that Jesus is for me, that he is by my side. He wants me free of shackles, standing on my own two feet, praising God, recovering my dignity as *mother* and *sister* (Luke 8:21) and as *daughter* (Luke 8:48; 13:16)—serving him (Luke 4:39), following him as disciple, and sharing my gifts with him (Luke 8:1–3). He is my only treasure and that is why my heart is with him (Luke 12:34).

It is a matter of giving birth today, here and now, to the Word of God. It is a matter of believing it is possible for God to enable all of us to give birth to a new Ursuline life, to a new society, which seems as impossible to be born as it was for old and sterile Elizabeth to give birth to John, and for young unwedded Mary to give birth to Jesus. The only way to lead a New Life is by daring to give birth to this New Life in whatever way the Lord wants me to give it to him. That is why, today, I am a Latin American Ursuline Woman on the Way.

A Work in Process

MARY CABRINI DURKIN, OSU

MARCH 26, 1954

Dear Anne,

Thank you for the pin you gave me for my birthday. Yes, Mother said I can skip Block Rosary to come to your house for your birthday. Isn't it weird how both our birthdays are in March? And next year we'll be teenagers. Cool! Do you get to pick your birthday dinner like I do? The pin will look great with my green sweater.

Sincerely yours,
Ellen

(1958)

Dear Anne,

Tell Tom to tell Bob that my dress has that pink sash. He thinks it's just white with those embroidered green leaves. Yeah, rosebuds would be neat. See you later.

Ellen

Dear Anne,

I'm going to be up in the pressroom with Jayne Ann and Sister Philip Neri, trying to get the headlines done for the front page. Come up when you finish with art—or your conversation with Sister Bernard Marie, whichever comes before the 4:40 bus home.

Ellen

(1959)

Anne–

Let's see whether Mother Catherine will let us out of this study hall. We can tell her we have to hear each other's Latin subjunctives for this afternoon's test. I'm dying to know what Bernard Marie said about Mother Helen's reaction when she told her we were *both* interested in the convent.

Ellen

A.

What do you mean you have to study chemistry instead? I'm *dying*.

E.

8–16/17–62

Dear Sister Anne,

A week ago, before retreat began, I was scared to death. The postulants were so excited, counting down to their reception. It just seemed too quick for August 17 to be our profession day too. Three years of novitiate looked awfully short, all of a sudden.

But now that it's the night before—no, the very day, well past midnight now—I'm deeply peaceful. I wish I could tap on your cell curtain and talk, the way we used to at night before we entered. It's Great Silence time, of course, even though you are in a cell just across the dorm. Still, I have to tell you how I've spent this night. Not asleep, of course. I could never sleep the night before Christmas or the first day of school. And remember my four sleepless nights before Reception Day? Then afterwards I cried the rest of the week because I didn't want to be a nun, especially after the senior novices cut my hair.

Anyway, tonight I've been talking with the women of my family who are in heaven, asking them to help me with the life ahead. Ellen Ames never forgot what famine meant, and always cared for the hungry, even when she couldn't really afford to. Ma Killoran fell in love with an Irish freedom fighter and passed that love of justice on to their children. Grandmother worked very, very hard, was courageous and dedicated when she was widowed young. And her mother had the guts not only to leave that brutal second husband of hers but also to write to the president for a share of his Civil War pension. She got it too! They're all the kind of brave, strong women that I'd like to take after. I'll need their help, and Mother Cabrini's.

When we were still in high school we used to talk about which of the vows we thought would be hardest for us. You used to say chastity. I said obedience. I still think that. Let's face it. I'm bossy. Sister John Nicholas says she used to think I was meek, before I entered, and then she saw how I really am. Part of it is from being the oldest in the family. Part of it is just me. My mother is always telling me how bad I am at listening to other people. With God's help, I'll strive to work hard on my imperfections, in the spirit of the vow. Would you help me by giving me a little nudge when I'm particularly bossy?

The most important thing is that God's love called me, and if He loves me so much, I want to give everything I can, every effort

I can, to be close to Him, so that nothing will stand in the way, like in the Song of Songs: "Wear me as a seal upon your heart, as a seal upon your arm; Many waters cannot quench love, no flood sweep it away."

Tomorrow morning—no, this morning—when we sing the "*Veni Creator Spiritus*," my deepest heart will be singing "*Accende lumen sensibus, Infunde amorem cordibus.*" And even though the vows we'll make are technically for three years, I know that between Him and me, they'll be for life.

Love in Christ,
Sister Mary Cabrini

WASHINGTON, D.C.
JULY 7, 1965

Dear Anne,

Thanks for your letter. I'm not too surprised to hear about your turmoil, since you felt so uncertain about your vocation a couple of years ago. I'm praying and praying for you, and doing special penances. I wish I weren't here at Catholic U. for the summer and we could talk in person. Even though you aren't sure about your vocation, I feel so sure for you. The juniorate has been horribly straining, of course, for all of us. At times I've looked around the refectory at the pill bottles and said to myself, "There's something wrong with this. We're all too young to need tranquilizers."

Just guessing, but I'd bet it never occurs to Mother Helen what stress she puts us under. But that's not religious life, just a temporary situation. And you must admit it brings us all close together, doesn't it?

I see your kindergartners pulling on your habit to show you their art work and know that you're a real mother to them, just the way Saint Angela told us to be. I know how you love them, because I love my sophomores too.

Please try to hang in there till we're out of the juniorate and can live our vocation in a more normal atmosphere. We'll all still be together, supporting each other in the Lord!

Thanks again for writing. Classes end August 5, and we'll be home the seventh. God bless you.

Love in Christ,
Cabrini

SAINT URSULA VILLA
SEPTEMBER 15, 1971

Dear ...,

When you dropped me off yesterday, we seemed to have said everything. But today, here I am wishing I could pick up the phone and reach you. I've always transmuted aspects of loving you into talk, haven't I? The phone is one of the strands between us that I know we have to loosen. I'm not really able to say "cut."

Loving you kind of crept up on me, but it's not going to creep away so easily. I was awfully naive and idealistic, to think that because I loved Jesus, I couldn't fall in love with anyone else. Not being Irish, you didn't suffer from that Jansenistic unbodiedness that I had such a dose of. Maybe you weren't so surprised. I hadn't expected the rush of physicality that you brought to life in me. Nor the anguish. Nor the joy. You surprised me, but not so much as I surprised myself.

By 1965, I had spent six years of novitiate and juniorate under glass trying to be—well, maybe not unnatural—supernatural? For me it amounted to nearly the same thing. After being submerged in an all-female world that long, then being the only woman at XU when it was still all male—no wonder my sexuality woke up all at once.

And there you were.

And there I was, about six years retarded; vowed in my heart, not just on paper, to lifelong chastity; and deeply immersed in you. A dilemma. A torment, really.

Funny thing—I never feel guilty about loving you. That makes this time even harder. What we've shared will always be real for me, and good. But if I start in on that topic, this will be the kind of letter it shouldn't be.

So—I'll probably see you at a civic meeting or somewhere and say, "Hi, how are things?" And you'll answer, "Fine, how about you?" And what will I say? I'll work on that one.

Love,
Cabrini

SAINT URSULA VILLA
MAY 3, 1972

Dear...,

What a relief to know that we could have lunch together yesterday without coming apart at the seams! I'm glad that you can still interpret me to myself when I was intangible about things like my vows. It felt deeply right to hear you say it so clearly, "It's as though you're monogamous with God." That's it. That's always been it.

Part of the pain has been knowing the goodness of all of this—me, you, the things that brought us together around social justice and literature, and our own spiritual journeys— but that still this form of love isn't, for me, the basis on which to build my life. It's all a matter of being true in the core of myself, somehow.

There's something I wanted to tell you at lunch yesterday and didn't. (Your faith struggles made me fear it wouldn't seem authentic to you.) There's just one person I've been talking with about us—Jesus. It's been the most helpful thing I've done in the past year. The months are getting better for me. You seemed that way too, and I'm glad.

Love,
Cabrini

INDIANA STATE U.
JUNE 12, 1978

Dear Germaine, Jerome, Judy, and Mary Alice,

Missing me yet? No, you're rejoicing that you don't have to wash my overbaked casserole dishes, right? How about Kaleb? Show him this letter and see whether he wags his tail.

I'm not sure whether this creative writing course will produce anything of value, but for me it—well, writing poetry takes me deeper than anything else, except prayer and love. Right now that's helpful, because a lot of things seem very dark to me and need sorting out. Is this the beginning of middle age? The older Sisters all tell me that thirty-seven is too young to be middle-aged. Maybe so. Maybe not.

As a break from writing I brought along *Trinity*, about the potato famine and the troubles, and *Love in the Urban Ghetto*. They make me even more aware of how little I am living the challenge of Vatican II to address the world's needs and realities with the Gospel. Yes, I'm involved in our neighborhood's housing needs and, of course, in trying to educate my students to work for justice. But what difference do I make, and how committed am I, really? I'm especially ashamed of the day, before I left to come here, when I was up at the convent and a woman came to the door for food. I filled some bags for her. Okay. But the only meat available was something that Sister Mary was going to use for supper that night, and I didn't want to undergo her wrath. So I sent that woman off without it because I wasn't willing to stick my neck out.

That day spilled over this week into a poem to my great-great-grandmother, Ellen Ames Conlan, sort of a prayer, really. She had been through Ireland's potato famine, then came to this country. She and her husband had a small grocery store, and in a recession in the 1870s, she bankrupted it by giving food away. Hearing her story from my mother is one of my earliest memories.

Would one of you please call Mrs. Curtis and tell her I won't be at the July Block Club meeting? I forgot to let her know. And tell her that if we need a place for the August meeting, I could host it at our house—I'll be home by then—if none of you sees a conflict in our household schedule. Thanks.

Mary Alice, thanks for the card I found waiting for me here. It felt good to find a "home voice." Already!

Love in Christ,
Cabrini

P.S. One of my classmates, who has relatives in Cincinnati, wants to visit there over the July Fourth weekend, and I'm going to ride back and forth with her Friday and Monday.

INDIANA STATE U.
JULY 6, 1978

Dear Elizabeth,

Your visit while I was home Sunday evening was really a shock. Back here at ISU, I still can't put it together. Being on the council these years with you as superior, I know you want us to move forward. So how, how, how, can you ask us to move back from Taft and Cleinview to the convent?

Yes, I heard you say that you want some of us in a formation household within the convent, to incorporate the new postulant. But closing the only place we've got to try something new for religious life? This is one of the few situations since the novitiate when my obedience doesn't see reason in the decision. And I must at least tell you why.

Living at Taft and Cleinview has been hard but happy.

Hard because we didn't know what we were doing. The five of us set out to take religious life into the neighborhood, into the world (à la Cardinal Suenens), to live our values in the context of ordinary life, not just walled away. (We didn't have one foot outside religious life, as a lot of the Sisters thought three years ago, when we asked to do this.) To tell the truth, in many ways we have recreated aspects of semi-monastic life because it's all we've known. Close though we've been for years, it was hard to develop a community life without any of the structures we were used to. But at least we were trying to make the structures more responsive to the realities of our apostolic life.

It has been happy for a lot of reasons. It has been exciting to draw on what we've been learning, especially through Sister Teresa Ledochowska's work on Saint Angela. Angela was engaged in the needs of her time, a woman of her own day. Her life was not so very different from the lives of other women, and her sisters lived among the people. Here we are more in touch with our neighbors and their needs and share in some of their struggles.

Getting to Taft and Cleinview, to that life, was not easy for me. A decade ago, after Vatican II, I could hardly wrench the "monastic me" open to fluid, less certain ways of being. Monasteries are supposed to separate people from the world to concentrate on God, and no doubt that works well for people who are already firmly mature. I—perhaps many of us—got separated from myself, with every minute of the day structured, with styles of prayer prescribed, with relationships controlled. Even though things have changed, moving to Saint Ursula feels like moving backward. I'm going to find it hard to fit there.

You say that you want us settled in before the postulant arrives. I'll be home August 10. The other Sisters in our house will no doubt work out a moving schedule for us.

See you then. Please pray for me.

Yours in Christ,
Cabrini

INDIANA STATE U.
JULY 8, 1978

Dear Mary Jerome, Judy, Mary Alice, and Germaine,

Well, I've had a little more time to sort out my feelings about our move—grim. Of course, we'll talk later. But I can't let this moment go by without saying to all of you what it has meant to me to be with you these three years.

Fun!

Deeper too. Maybe the biggest thing has been just passing our little prayer room at odd hours of the day or evening and seeing one or another of you sitting there. Now that we don't all get up at the same time and meditate together, etc., just that presence says volumes about prayer in our lives and is the greatest support to my own prayer. It's something I've needed. Lately I've been trying to let the Holy Spirit do more of the work when I pray, instead of thinking I have to run things. Sometimes there seems to be a vast empty space. But hanging in there—well, you all know that for me it has meant finding in the Spirit the feminine face of God, and knowing that I'm the stuff of God and God's the stuff of me—of us women.

Thanks for all of it, for sharing your dedication to Catholic education in your different schools, for supporting me when I dressed up like Saint Angela to fasten the Equal Rights Amendment to the cathedral door on Women's Equality Day, for the parties we've had, and on and on.

See you August 10. Hey, I wonder if we could pack up household things and store them in a basement at the convent till maybe sometime—no, when—another small household takes shape in the future. Would you ask Elizabeth about that, please? It would make the dark parts of this a little brighter.

Love in Christ,
Cabrini

ST. URSULA CONVENT
MARCH 27, 1979

Dear Lou,

I hadn't intended to intrude upon your sabbatical, knowing how single-minded you Jesuits are. But there's something I just have to share with you. You know from our talks last year how I have been wrestling with this hunger issue and its meaning for me. You know I've never been able to forgive myself for letting that woman go away without meat last summer, even if you could give me absolution for it.

Recently, I saw a flyer for a Bread for the World organizing internship—go to NY for training, then come back and develop local action. I admire BFW's Gospel base and intelligent, systemic action. The Cincinnati chapter is pretty meager, though there are a few committed members. So I was wondering about doing this internship and getting things going here.

Last Saturday, after morning Mass, the student receptionist here at the convent didn't show up, and I had to cover till she rolled out of bed and got here. Since I had planned to pray at that time, considering this BFW thing, I was annoyed but settled down with Matthew 25. Then the doorbell rang. Annoyed again! It was a grungy but cheery old guy who wanted to rake leaves in exchange for something to eat. A good stiff March wind made that a self-defeating project, but he insisted. So—get some food together for him. I couldn't leave the switchboard unattended. The solution seemed to be recruiting a sister to take over while I packed food. Could I bother someone else? As it turned out, Ruth Ann was good enough to do it with no complaint.

By the time I was back with sandwiches, etc., the man had given up on the raking. We stood on the porch for a while. He was very interested in my crucifix, affable, chatty. Eventually, he gestured to a grocery cart on the driveway in which he seemed to have all his possessions.

"Would you like some wine?" he asked. "I've got some wine in there."

It was a little early in the a.m. for me to imbibe, so I declined, and we parted on friendly terms. I settled back down with my Bible, to try to recover from this interruption.

Interruption? I looked at the page. "I was hungry and you gave me something to eat." Then it hit me, so hard that I said it out loud: "He offered me wine! That man offered me wine!" And I knew that Jesus had come to forgive me. This doesn't have to be about apparitions. That was Jesus the wino, Jesus in the wino. It doesn't matter.

Needless to say, I signed up for the BFW internship. Thank God, I think that now I can do it freely, instead of out of guilt. This is going to be exciting!

Sorry that this letter is so full of me. Meanwhile, I hope that you are having a wonderfully enriching semester. Don't take the time to reply to this. I'll see you in June.

In Christ,
Cabrini

SAINT URSULA CONVENT
JUNE 30, 1979

Dear Anne,

Thanks for your hospitality when I was in New York. It meant a lot to me to be in your home. Bill's wonderful. You two are so well matched! Joannie is darling. She's already shown good taste in parents.

The way you and Bill are giving yourselves to the poor in your parish, especially through the school, is a deep inspiration to me. You're sacrificing so much, creating your home in the midst of that poverty. It's got to be burdensome, but you both seem cheerful.

After you left the convent, we both had a hard time knowing how to be with each other in a new way. I felt as though a part of me had been sliced out. Sometimes in the middle of a grammar lesson (it's hard to pay attention to those, even for the teacher), I'd find a horrible emptiness welling up in me. Or something would happen and I'd think, "I've got to tell Anne about this." Or I'd recall something and want to say, "Remember when we....?" You won't be surprised that I'm still doing bits of poetry about how I feel:

That year,
like an empty house,
stands among the weeds
of memory.

Since then, we've had lots of painful practice in separation and loss: John Nicholas, Philip Neri, Bernard Marie, Barb, Linda, and Lynda, to name a few. For me, the hardest came first.

Well, being with you last week was a special grace. We've been friends. We've been sisters. Maybe we can be friends again.

Love in Christ,
Ellen

PORT AU PRINCE, HAITI
JULY 10, 1984

Dear Irma, Kyle, and BFW friends,

Greetings from Haiti, and from our Saint Ursula volunteer group. The poverty here is almost overwhelming to us. So is the warmth of many Haitians to us. Work with the Missionaries of Charity cuts right down to the bone. There will be volumes to share with you, but till I return, just this one snapshot from the Undernourished Children's Home: Gerald, six months, six pounds. His whole torso fits in my one hand. His ribs ripple against my palm when he laughs. These kids have no business laughing, but they do. Someone asked me whether our BFW work on public policy isn't pretty remote compared to these urgent, immediate needs. I feel the opposite. I can only push porridge at the Home. With BFW I/we can hope to prevent some of these kids from being here at all. See you at the August meeting.

                    In Christ,
                    Cabrini

STATION AVENUE
JUNE 29, 1988

Dear Donna,

You've been on my mind these last two weeks since Father's Day. It must have been painful for you. I couldn't call that day, though I was praying for you.

It was good to have you staying with us in those days around your father's death.

I called Shelly in Jersey and Marianne in Chicago, since both had wanted to know when your dad died. And, of course, Mary. (Did she bring any of her daughters to the funeral home? I wanted you to meet Becca, the one who's my god-daughter. It always gives me joy to see school ties still intact. Part of what we tried to do for you—establish a community experience that was authentic—worked.

I admit to being prejudiced about the class of '69, still my favorite. I had some significant segment of the 108 of you each year. The "Spanish group" were my freshman homeroom, all very dear, but especially that closely knit bunch that came from Holy Name School. Their English class was my only one that year, when I was trying to be a full-time graduate student too. And run the school newspaper, of course.

Do you remember that I had you for English II in the late morning; then you had a study hall supervised only by Carol Blum (class president that year), who said "Shut up, you guys!" at about forty-five-second intervals for almost an hour? Then you went to lunch, but of course there wasn't enough room for all of you in the cafeteria, so they cut your lunchtime down to twenty minutes and sent you back up to me for seventy minutes of Latin II. Sophomores! What a debacle! Every time I see someone from that group, I hear another tale of who was shut in which classroom cupboard, or hanging out the window watching the Sacred Mushroom Band doing their flower child things across the street.

The next year, in American Lit, Chris McCarthy bawled me out in class one day for talking over everybody's head and not using the blackboard enough. She was right, of course. I had just wound up my master's and you were the victims. Meanwhile, you and Shelly and Mary and I just about lived in that hotbox on the third floor that we called a pressroom for your junior and senior years. We had that mini-refrigerator and a service sink and—didn't we have a cot? How did I survive moderating the newspaper and the yearbook and Black Student Union, along with a full load of Latin and English? And loving it! Now that I've been out of the classroom for a couple of years, I miss it so much that I often wander through the lunchroom, getting my "kid fix."

All along, I was hearing Jesus say, "If I be lifted up, I shall draw all things to myself." I had been drawn, at least partly, through my sophomore religion teacher's helping me get to know him. (That was Sister Ignatius.) I wanted to help my students sense that magnetism too.

But I don't think I could have handled the extracurriculars except for seeing my editors and officers developing skills for leadership and community. The world was starting to get exciting for women in the sixties.

What really brought me close to your class was the times. You had all the sixties issues, and so did we in the community after Vatican II. My silent pledge to myself was not to meet your questions with panacea solutions, but to enter into them with you. I was just discovering that my old answers weren't sufficient for me, either. Once Marianne got mad at me for not having the remedy for whatever her malaise was at the time, after she had plucked up the courage to talk about it. Since I was The Nun, I was supposed to have the answers.

Well, here we are all these years later, and I still don't have them. You said on the phone when we talked that you find it hard to get a conversation with God started up again. I don't have a recipe for that. But one of my favorite Gospel lines is from the father who says to Jesus, "Lord, I believe. Help thou my unbelief." The great thing is, that was enough for Jesus. I depend on that a lot.

God bless you, Donna.

Love in Christ,
Cabrini

STATION AVENUE
MAY 15, 1988

Dear Anne,

A couple of days ago I saw Mark, and he gave me the good news that Bill is doing well in response to his radiation treatments. Thank God! What a terrible diagnosis to walk into when you got back from Germany!

You've been on my mind also because I recently saw at the Villa a tree that Mark and his family had planted there in memory of your mother. How I loved her! Among her many gifts, she was a very astute lady. I remember some remarks she made when we were kids about my intensity. Good Lord! How right she was! Too intense, too young.

How very much too young we were to enter! *We* is a beautiful word to me still. But it's easy to see now that my immaturity led to overidentifying with the community and all the structure that went with it in those monastic days. How rigid I became in the framework of all the supposedly "religious" ways to do and be! Maybe some of that will be in me forever. It's certainly something I have to struggle with still.

I regret—I'm really sorry—how unable I was to respond to you outside that framework, when your own self and vocation were taking you in a different and healthy direction.

My prayers for Bill continue. Will you be in Cincinnati in the foreseeable future? Please call.

Love in Christ,
Ellen

STATION AVENUE
MAY 27, 1989

Dear Rosemary,

Whether as an Ursuline or as an alumna, you would have loved this afternoon's celebration in honor of Sister Mary Helen's retirement! I'm still excited about how well it all went off, and how touched we all were, from the freshmen to the oldest alumna there in the auditorium. The program was chiefly a series of tributes, one per decade of her involvement in Saint Ursula, by alums of those decades, plus three current students. They were realistic, funny, touching. There had been no script or directives, but several threads kept appearing— Sister Mary Helen's treatment of her students as individuals, her empowerment of young women, and her concern for their families. We interspersed all that with presentations and with off-stage voices rendering the Prologue to *The Canterbury Tales* and the witches' scene in *Macbeth*-everybody's favorite memories from her English IV classes.

Elizabeth had put into albums the mountain of letters and cards that alumnae had sent in secretly for her. It was a fitting tribute for someone who has been the spiritual and professional leader here for many of those decades. She carried it off with panache!

· Sister Mary Helen represents for me the best of what we've given young women here since 1910. Now, while we're planning for lay trusteeship of the school, this event sums up a lot of life for us who've been involved in the high school. There will be some major letting go, which our sisters in the parochial schools have already had to do over the last years. I know that will be hard for me, since—God forgive me—I always think I know what's best. Just like my mother—also the eldest in her family. That's scary, no matter how much I admire her.

Today highlights the difference between now and a time in the seventies when I looked over the community and saw no one I wanted to grow to be like. Now I see so many wonderful women. Have they changed? Have I? Maybe we all have. Maybe I can see more now. Which is not to say that I want to live the life they've lived. If we don't create a new life, there won't be any. But I understand now that their goodness is a foundation stone of whatever that future will be.

We didn't learn much of anything about Saint Angela before the seventies, and here are Saint Ursula "girls" from as far back as the twenties experiencing her charism through Sister Mary Helen. Charism is mysterious, isn't it? It was in there all the time, passed on in ways that we couldn't even articulate. When we did express it in a mission statement a few years ago, we were really drawing out of our lives and hearts. I think it's a sort of spiritual genetics, and we self-selected as we unconsciously found in the community something that was also—all unawares—inside ourselves.

It's happening with our associate members, the Companions, you know. But do you realize how many years it's been since we had our last postulant, Louise? Ten. Since she left, Margie's actually the last one to enter and stay—twenty-five years ago. The Spirit is trying to say *something*.

What is the call of this moment? We've been through the monastic way of life and a more apostolic, ministry-oriented model. Perhaps, as we hand on our schools, we are to address together the needs and disempowerment of women in new ways, for those who are not being served. Or will tomorrow's Ursulines live their consecration as Angela's first Company did, each in the context of her own family, neighborhood, and work? When you think about it, Angela created a form of consecrated life that resembled nothing else known as religious life in her day: no convents, no habits, no common works, mainly a Gospel presence in their world and a special concern for young women. I know that oversimplifies, but it's the basic outline.

When will you be in Cincinnati? I'll leave June 20 for the Dante seminar in Italy. Thank heaven, Daddy is well cared for at the Alzheimer Center; I can leave with peace of mind about him and Mother. You know, she's losing her vision. It must be hard for you to live away with your parents in such a fragile state too. I know you'll be doing a lot for them while you're in Cincinnati. However, if you're in before June 20, Margie and I would love to have you come here to our house for dinner. We're both decent cooks. Naw! We're great!

Love in Christ,
Cabrini

STATION AVENUE
JUNE 7, 1989

Dear Rosemary,

It's good to know that we'll connect before I leave. Margie and I hope that you can come for that dinner on the seventeenth. We'll count on it unless we hear otherwise from you.

Your note asked what we *do* at our Companions' gatherings. There isn't one absolute constant, unless it would be refreshments. You probably know that there are about ten laymen and laywomen and three Sisters (Mary Jerome, Mary Anne, and I) who participate. We all take turns, in pairs, leading a time of prayer or reflection. The constant, I guess, is that Saint Angela's spirituality, the special quality of her relationship with God and others, touches each of us. (She said to have a good time together, so that fits with the refreshments too, doesn't it?) We talk about our month or our jobs or our families, in that context. That's mostly what we do—

share our lives and faith and get from one another encouragement, insight, just the support of prayer together. Whether it's Kathleen's painful back, Paul and Carol's young adult children, Mary Jerome's parishioners, they all come into our circle. You've been here to see that the Companions participate in community feast days and special events too.

Having Saint Angela reflected from a lay perspective makes her live afresh for those of us who have been Ursulines for years. The presence of men in our Companionship—brothers in the spirit—is a new and very fulfilling relationship for me. Our Ursuline family is growing! We need all of us, and more.

We'll see you on the seventeenth.

Love in Christ,
Cabrini

STATION AVENUE
SEPTEMBER 14, 1989

Dear Ron,

When we parted in Assisi, I told you something of what this summer meant to me. It will be a long time before the whole of that is clear. Dante/the Comedy wasn't just an academic course. It was a sacred journey—sixteen of us on it together those six weeks...Siena, Assisi, Rome, Ravenna, Florence. Did you know how powerful it would be as we all brought our diverse personal journeys into this context?

How can I thank you for admitting me to the course? Among the blessings was that you are the kind of teacher who could assign a journal and I could write from my deepest core without inhibition, knowing a kindred spirit would be reading it.

On the other hand, maybe I would have anyway. Middle age is liberating, isn't it? ["*Nel mezzo del camin di nostra vita.*"] I think it's the time of the Spirit, at least for me. Here are a few lines that come out of my Druid ancestry, no doubt.

> *Trees listen to the Spirit's voice*
> *And repeat in rustle, whisper, sigh:*
> *Glossalia of maple, oak, and pine.*
> *What must it be to hear that voice?*
> *Let me melt to earth*
> *And rise through root*
> *To know her wordless Word.*

I'm just beginning to "unpack" that long weekend I took in Desenzano and Brescia. You asked whether it was worth the four trains each way. I said yes, of course. I want to let you see why because I'm so grateful for this too. A few glimpses, at least:

— a riveting hour before the coffin and remains of Saint Angela, the intensity of her presence, my prayer there for each of my sisters at home and for all of us together

— yearning beyond words in Angela's bedroom, where she must have sought God's guidance so often in birthing her Company; I kissed the floor and long pressed my hand to the original bare bricks of the wall

— peaceful reassurance in the Merici house in LeGrezze, outside Desenzano; I have worried about how we are to refound the Ursuline reality for today, ordinary as we are, and realized that her experiences and preparation here were ordinary too

— tiny elderly ladies, Daughters of Angela, who hosted me in Brescia with all the warm solicitude of great-aunts

— a German Ursuline, who volunteered to spend a day guiding me around Desenzano, connecting through our meager Italian and our Ursuline kinship

— the great canvases of Moretto, beauty in the service of spirit, including Angela's spirit, I believe

— the stones on which she walked, a very real woman in a very real world, making sense of it and her place in it as best she could, all in the context of God's total and embracing love

Sounds like Dante, doesn't it? Well, ultimately we're all on the same pilgrimage. Thank you. Thank you.

Love in Christ,
Cabrini

DESENZANO, ITALY
MAY 10, 1991

Dear Ron,

In Italy again, and thinking of you, once more with gratitude. My side trip to Brescia in 1989 catalyzed an interest that developed into a study I've called "Art in Brescia, the Charism of Angela Merici, and Women's Leadership Today." I've just presented it at an inter-Ursuline general superiors' conference in Rome. The international, intercontinental, intercultural experience is expanding my Ursuline horizons hugely. There is a great kinship of spirit threading through our widely different ways of being daughters of Angela. The conference includes two days here.

Another update—in March I was elected superior of my community for the next six years, starting in June. Despite—

or because of—our small size (35), it's frightening, as my dreams during the last two months attest. One of my very deepest prayers is that my flaws and inadequacies may not stand in the way of what the community will need, of God's work in the Sisters. I believe God can manage.

I wouldn't be able to face this if it were not that part of the preelection process surfaced the comment, "She will lead us down new paths." The community's openness to electing someone of whom they can say that means that there is a readiness in us for something new. I don't pretend to know what that is.

What has come to me here is that, as a community, we need to come to Desenzano and Brescia to seek a closer contact with Saint Angela, to answer that question for ourselves. Sister Mary Jerome, our current superior, is also on this trip and has encouraged me in this notion, which I'll present to the community at our Chapter assembly in June: a community pilgrimage in 1993. We can't afford it, but if God calls us to this, as I believe, and Saint Angela is leading us, the funds will come, from heaven.

Yesterday we were at Mass in Brescia at the Church of Saint Angela, site of her remains. Just after receiving the Lord, I had a sense that all of my life had led up to that moment and would flow forth from it. That was accompanied by an overpowering sweetness—not a popular word in today's spirituality, perhaps, or mine, but very real for me then.

Please pray for me and for all of us. Give my fond greetings to Kathe and Bill.

Love in Christ,
Cabrini

STATION AVENUE
JULY 20, 1993

Dear Ruth Ann, Margie, Mary Alice, and Elizabeth,

After the experience we have just had on pilgrimage, won't it be hard to sit down to a week of council meetings on Monday? But—enclosed you will find a draft agenda. We all know that the time has come to bite the bullet of our Chapter '91 resolution that by 1995 we will decide which road to set out on: dissolution, merger, or new form(s) of our Ursuline life. Next week we will have to outline steps toward that decision.

In case you're as scared as I am, let's listen together to Saint Angela's counsel to the women to whose hands she entrusted the spiritual leadership of the Company: "Do not lose courage, then, if you feel yourselves incapable of knowing and doing all that such a special charge demands....Act, bestir yourselves, have hope and confidence, make efforts, cry to him with all your hearts. You will certainly see wonders, if you direct everything to the praise of his divine Majesty and the greater good of souls....You must understand that I am more alive now than I was when on earth, and I see better and hold dear all the good works that I see you constantly performing, and I intend to help you and am able to help you more, and serve you well in every way."

See you Monday!

Love,
Cabrini

STATION AVENUE
JULY 13, 1994

Dear Barbara,

You're a brave woman! When you become a novice next month, you'll be setting out with the rest of us as an Ursuline of Cincinnati on a very new path. What a providence that you could be a part of the preparation for this journey! You walked with us the streets of Brescia, prayed with us at the side of Saint Angela, participated in the reflection leading up to last month's Chapter meetings, joined in Chapter discussions.

Surely sisters told you how the Chapters of the last twenty-five years created reams of paper, and decision after decision. There was a peace in us when we affirmed the single sentence to come out of this one: "We, the Ursulines of Cincinnati, commit ourselves to co-create our future and to re-found our community under the inspiration of the Holy Spirit, in response to the signs of the times, by being open to and nurturing new forms of Ursuline life rooted in Saint Angela's vision of the original Company." And there was a holy awe as we all signed our names to it.

That doesn't mean that we have no fear, nor that we really know the depth of what that commitment will mean. I admire your courage for joining us on this continuation of our pilgrimage, "journeying toward light" as an Ursuline.

We may be very small, but there is a joyful sisterhood among us, along with differences and stresses. We like one another, by and large. We are learning to go deeper with one another.

The "Caleb Party," our dreaming, studying, visioning, future-scouting group, has learned something together in the last three years. The most significant learning we have to offer the community is not plans but this: the binding force at

the core of our future may be found in our sharing of ourselves, of faith and prayer, of our relationship with and in
God. Mary Alice, Germaine, Mary Anne, Elizabeth, Margie,
Rose Angela, and I—so different—experience this as a powerful unity among ourselves and with Saint Angela.

My own trust has been inspired by the spiritual freedom
of our eldest sisters. It seems that they are willing to let go,
not to need to control the future which will evolve in and
through new members, through women like you whose para-
digm of consecrated life may be very different, formed in a
consciousness—a whole world-view—unlike that of my gen-
eration. You say that you have found in these elders encouragement for your own Ursuline vocation. It's on their shoulders that we stand.

We'll all be depending together on Saint Angela's promise that she will be with us, seeing, helping, "with my Lover,
or rather, the Lover of each one of us, provided that they
have faith and do not lose courage and hope."

Welcome! God bless you, God bless us all!

Love in Christ,
Cabrini

Between Two Worlds

HEDWIG OWSIAK, OSU

*Hold them all in your love and bear with them all
equally…after that, leave it to God; he will do marvelous
things.*
　　　　　　　　　　—SAINT ANGELA, EIGHTH COUNSEL

Heddie Owsiak was the eighth member of our group. She
would have been awarded the prize for traveling the greatest
distance, for as superior general of the Tildonk Congregation
of Ursulines, her usual residence was Brussels. Heddie's Eu-
ropean background made her our most traveled and, in many
ways, our most experienced participant. But more than that
Heddie was gifted with kindness, compassion, and understanding that endeared her to us all.

But where, then, is her journey story? Not here. Not here
because the period of contemplative reflection essential for
such a task was a luxury Heddie was not permitted. We had
hardly settled in to our writing when Heddie was pulled beyond the circle. Three months earlier, on April 5, the presi-
dents of Rwanda and Burundi had been killed in a plane crash.
With their deaths—declared "assassination" by their en-
emies—the country exploded. Zaire, just west of Rwanda,
became a refuge for tens of thousands of terrified fleeing
people. It was in the little town of Goma, just over the border
from Rwanda, that the Tildonk Ursulines had a community.

Newspapers carried the horror of the massacres day after
day, but no newspaper account could move us as powerfully

as the anguish that Heddie experienced as she tried desperately far into the night to find out what was happening in Goma. Under such tension there was no possibility for the quiet time necessary for a journey story. That she stayed with us through the month, bringing her notes to our sharing sessions, trying to quiet her heart in its turmoil, listening to our stories, responding, encouraging, was in itself a grace for all of us. When, at the end of the month, Heddie left us, it was to fly to Zaire as soon as possible.

From August to November we heard nothing, but on November 7, I received a four-page fax from Belgium. Heddie had been to Goma; she had experienced its horrors; she had witnessed unspeakable cruelty and felt the humiliation of finding herself powerless.

That four-page fax is in a way Heddie's journey story for time is, after all, relative, and a few weeks can shake us and shape us as well as a decade. So here is Heddie's story.

I left for Zaire on September 4 and only arrived back here [Brussels] on October 18. Three days late and after some hair-raising and expensive experiences in Kinshasa trying to get a ticket. Right now I am preparing to leave for India (November 15) to be with our International Renewal Program which will last until just before Christmas. If all goes well, I shall arrive back on December 21. So much for the broad outline of these past months.

Really, it is difficult to put into writing all that I experienced in Zaire. There was such a mixture of hope and despair in all the events during my stay. Hope because of the joy-filled religious profession of two young Zairese Ursulines…and situations of despair which are visible everywhere in Goma.

I spent much time listening to the "stories" told by our young sisters—they are so young, just professed or novices or postulants. They have, however, lived a lifetime in the past months since the plane crash on April 6 which precipitated all the agonizing events since then. I have yet to put together my reflections on it all. I can't get the immensity of it all out of my heart or head.

I visited one of the children's camps. People say that there are more than 4,000 children there, which I believe. The children are beginning to look healthy again; but what of their future? These are children who are totally alone in the world (or seemingly so), although from time to time one or another mother comes searching for her child and is lucky enough to find him or her. One such mother came to our convent with her two children. They had been cared for by our sisters, nursed back to mental and physical health, and eventually brought to the camp by UNICEF workers. Somehow this mother found the children. The older boy wanted to come back to tell our sisters and to show them his mother This was one of the stories on the side of hope.

I met another mother who had been a refugee in the first wave coming into Goma; later, relying on the word of the new government that it was safe to return to Rwanda, she went back home—only to be confronted shortly thereafter with a total massacre in their village. Her husband was brutally killed by machetes; and she gave terrible descriptions of the violence that goes on and one. Militia groups were simply brutal, cutting off the breasts of the women, not sparing the children. Somehow this woman escaped and fled to Goma for the second time, again a refugee. She arrived with some cloth to cover her body but with nothing to cover her infant child. Once the baby had had a little food, he simply laughed. I thought to myself how little he knows of the reality of his present situation and of the future.

I spent a great deal of time listening to the young sisters and those in initial formation. I spent time with the sick—two of our sisters came down with serious malaria—and visited some of the areas where people are encamped. Rwandan refugees themselves are helping in the camps; for they know the language which is totally different from the Swahili of Zaire. Fortunately, some of our young sisters know the language and could assist the refugees in an effective way.

The refugee camps are all along the roads, patrolled by military, both authentic and those pretending to be military. Aid workers are dwindling now which gives the false impression that the crisis is over. Some are leaving because the defeated Rwandan military is taking over the distribution of food, etc., by force. Those in need are being deprived of necessary supplies of food and medicine. Yet in Rwanda the massacres go on in the interior where they go undetected by United Nations Commission on Human Rights.

So much is the fruit of past colonization or of profit-taking by the greater powers of the world (Belgium, France, USA). Belgium pitted Tutsis and Hutus against each other; today the country doesn't know where to stand officially. On the human level, its very painful for the people of these tribes.

Our sisters suffer deeply from the conflict and try not to hurt one another. For a brief moment while I was there, they could take their time and really probe the depths of what they had lived and experienced without being able or having the time to articulate it. Their soul-searching is profound and painful. But they are trying to live the communion that those around them are often not able to accept as a value.

Imagine one sister who shared with me her journey in discovering what it really means to be a Tutsi; when the Tutsis are being accused of slaughtering innocent Hutus out of revenge. Really, I have to admit that I wept with many of the sisters, just listening to them, trying to share their pain but also the tremendous graces they have received.

I see that I'm already on page three of this fax. I trust that you will receive it soon—wherever you are. I can't promise I'll be in touch before I leave for India—there are so many matters that need to be resolved these days. I haven't forgotten our summer; in fact it was a wonderful grace and preparation for the pilgrimage to Zaire. Somehow I just can't put things on paper at this moment since I'm between two worlds and two pilgrimages. As I read over the small bits and pieces of my story which I put on paper at the end of our sessions in July, I find that they only prepared my heart for what I saw, felt, heard, experienced, lived, in Zaire for nearly seven weeks.

Don't think that I have abandoned the ship! I simply could not stop to write when the need among our sisters in Zaire was crying out for me to be a supportive presence. I believe that Angela is in the midst of all this somehow leading me and preparing me and my heart...for what, I'm not sure.

I still hope to meet you in the near future...but when? or how? When I get back from India I will try to look at the long-term schedule. Take care. Know that I appreciate you very much.

With love and gratitude,

Heddie

Where Angela Has Led

IRENE MAHONEY, OSU

*Tell them that now I am more alive than I was when they saw
me in the flesh, and that now I see them and know them better,
and can and want to help them more.*

–SAINT ANGELA, FIFTH COUNSEL

When Sister Diane Baumunk stood before an assembly
of Crow Indians in Montana to be formally adopted as a member of an Indian family, gifted with traditional beaded moccasins, earrings, and a dance shawl—and with a tribal mother
to guide her; when Sister Rose-Anne Engel rose in a court-
room of Calgary, Canada, as legal counsel for a woman who
was at last bringing charges against her husband after years
of physical abuse—there may well have been those in the community—both the civic and the religious community—who
looked on in bewilderment if not in disapproval. What had
happened to the Ursuline nuns, those cloistered women, se-
questered behind their convent walls, and hidden behind yards
of serge and linen?

On the surface the change was so radical that there was
good cause for bewilderment. One person, however, who
would not have had a moment's disapproval—or even legiti-
mate surprise—would have been Angela Merici, who had
founded the Ursulines more than four hundred fifty years
before.

When Angela drew her small company together in 1535,
she erected no monastery and constructed no walls; she left

the doors wide open. Although she had had a "vision," she was not, strictly speaking, a "visionary." Neither was she a prophet. She made no pretense of predicting what was to come. The future of her Company was unknown to her, and she made no effort to constrict it or control it. There lay her genius. Times would change, customs would change, needs would change. Her daughters, she counseled, should be able to perceive the changes and adjust their sights to meet them.

The official founding of the Company had taken place on November 25, 1535, when Angela and twenty-eight young women of Brescia, a city in northern Italy, attended Mass at the Church of Saint Afra and afterward gathered in the Oratory (a room placed at Angela's disposal by her longtime friend Isabetta Prato) to inscribe their names in a simple book which would act as register for the Company.

The ceremonial—even this word is too elaborate—could not have been more simple. The women who signed their names—or made their mark next to their name—were to have nothing visible to distinguish them. They would wear no religious habit; they would simply dress modestly, refraining from the ribbons and lace and jeweled ornaments which were part of the high style of the Italian Renaissance and the delight of their Brescian contemporaries. They would take no vows; rather they would follow privately, according to their conscience and the inspiration of the Holy Spirit, the virtues consonant with a life of dedicated virginity. Should they be inspired to make a private vow of chastity, they were free to do so. But this vow had no specific formula nor did it in any way differentiate members of the Company. And, of course, most shocking of all, they would be enclosed in no monastery; instead they would continue to live in their own homes or, in the case of those who were servants, in the houses of their employers.

What unpredictable thing had Angela Merici done? And what did she hope this unprecedented manner of life would accomplish? She had simply gathered about her a "Company of Women"—the phrase is scriptural, reminding us of those first women of the Gospels, that largely anonymous company who cast in their lot with Jesus, following him, listening to him, and ministering to him in whatever way he needed. Angela's hope was perhaps not appreciably different from this. She hoped to create a group of women whose single and determining purpose was to belong heart and soul to Jesus Christ, to live in such a way that their lives would speak of Christ, to support one another in their desires, and to serve the Gospel in whatever way they could.

For Angela, after long years of prayerful living, to live solely for Jesus Christ was a simple thing. It needed so little beyond a dedicated spirit, a will to persevere—and, of course, the ineffable grace which alone could make such living possible. Surely it did not need the massive, and often forbidding, structure of monasteries, the elaborate discipline of cloistered life. Such a way of life she recognized as hallowed by the sanction of the Church and by years of experience, but she was certain that God did not ordain it as the only way for those who wished a life of consecration.

Angela herself, despite her passionate dedication to Jesus Christ which had moved her to a life of austerity and contemplative prayer, had never felt drawn to either the life of the cloister or to marriage—the only approved choices for young women of her time. And so with quiet grace, without fanfare or trumpet, Angela inaugurated a way of life which would enable those with a sincere desire to live a life of consecration. Dowries or family status or personal abilities had nothing to do with it. Her Company of Women was all-inclusive. Did you wish to belong to Jesus Christ? Could you promise to obey, to the best of your ability and the grace you were given, the simple Rule she had drawn up? There were no other considerations. The Rule was demanding but simple to grasp. All of it was focused on Angela's single goal: total and joyous dedicated virginity.

These virgins were not shielded from the world by monastery walls. They walked the streets of Brescia; they attended Mass not in private chapels but in public churches. They lived among their kinsfolk, asking no special privileges or cutting themselves off from the life of their families. Some worked as domestics, obeying their mistresses like any servants, accepting their wages, responsibly fulfilling the tasks they were paid to do. Angela, well aware that such a life was not without its dangers, warned her daughters against the seductive influences around them, cautioning them against lingering on street corners, engaging in gossiping conversations in church, being influenced by those for whom jewelry and fancy headdresses were of prime importance, listening too impressionably to preachers with new untried ideas. But having warned them, she trusted them. She trusted them not because she was naive about human weakness but because she had an unshakable belief that the firm desire to belong solely to Jesus Christ was as sure a protection against "the world" as any monastery wall.

While Angela lived, her strong charismatic spirit and her reputation for holiness protected her Company. But within five years of her founding of the Company, Angela was dead. No doubt she felt she had left the Company protected, by giving it a Rule and spiritual instructions referred to as her Counsels and her Testament. She had also taken the precaution of appointing her successor: Lady Lucrezia Lodrone.

It is true, as one of Angela's commentators notes, that there is always a difficult period between the charismatic—even mystical—moment of the foundress' inspiration and the inevitable institutionalization of her dream. In Angela's case, however, the period was more than difficult; it was a firestorm that came close to destroying the Company. What happened between Angela's death (1540) and the final reconciliation between hostile factions of the Company (1560) is of a Byzantine complexity.

Suffice it to say that by the time these diverse elements were finally reunited, the face of the Company had already begun to change. A movement toward a distinguishing dress could be seen in the adoption of a leather cincture and the veletta (a small triangular piece of material worn around the shoulders). By 1580—contrary to Angela's initial vision—her daughters were wearing a common dress—or "habit." In time, some members found it increasingly difficult to live in their own homes (a development that Angela had foreseen), and thus common dwellings were established which enabled several members to live together.

In essence, however, Angela's Rule remained in place. The clerical suspicion and opposition directed against this "untried" way of life—a way that, in one sense, gave women far greater freedom than the Church or society had previously endorsed—was modified by a papal decree which made the Company an institute of Pontifical Right. Local bishops soon discovered that these dedicated women were very useful. They needed little and provided a great deal. They needed no monastery—at most a small house accommodating three or four would do. They were not dependent upon either the Church or the state for their livelihood; they maintained themselves in the simplicity of life which their Rule required and offered themselves freely in service to their neighbor and the Church. At a time when the Council of Trent was strongly recommending the religious education of the faithful, the members of the Company were identified as ideal for the teaching of Christian doctrine.

Gradually such companies sprang up in many Italian cities, initiated by bishops who had heard of their success in Brescia. Unlike the later proliferation of religious houses, where members of one community were sent to found another, these companies sprang up quite independently. Often these new groups did not have Angela's initial Rule but developed their own models based on the original structure. Even the name of Angela was sometimes forgotten, although the basic pattern of lifestyle and service remained constant.

Throughout the next two hundred years, the Italian foundations continued to spread and maintain Angela's original vision. In countries to the north, however, a very different pattern would emerge. In less than fifty years after Angela's death, the Company found its way into France. In 1592, in the little town of Isle-sur-Sorgues, not far from the city of Avignon in the province of Provence, the local bishop gave to a group of young women "wishing to serve God and neighbor," a rule appropriate to their desires and which he considered would provide them with a certain structure and stability. The rule was that used in the northern Italian city of Ferrara and was happily close to the Rule Angela had given her daughters.

This "unusual" way of life was a perfect fit for a country just recovering from the spiritual poverty consequent upon the brutal Wars of Religion that had ravaged France during the second half of the sixteenth century. Soon small groups of women, living in simple dedication to Jesus Christ and engaged in teaching Christian doctrine to the people of the region, developed throughout France. For the first few years the custom of living in their own homes continued, but for some groups it began to seem preferable to live together, sharing a common dwelling.

Observing the rapid and successful expansion of these groups, it comes as a shock to find that within twenty-five years from their founding most of them had undergone such radical change that they were well-nigh unrecognizable. The simple companies—without cloister or vows—had been transformed into monasteries.

What had happened? Clearly the change had been initiated by outside forces—notably the hierarchy, attempting to implement the reforms mandated by the Council of Trent: regularizing religious life, correcting its abuses, and returning it to its high spiritual purpose. Unfortunately, this "high spiritual purpose" was equated by many with the traditional, monastic forms of religious life. Whether the religious themselves not only conceded to but actively endorsed this momentous change is difficult to determine. In any case, such reforms, necessary and commendable in themselves, changed radically the way of life Angela had initiated. The simple Company of Saint Ursula, inaugurated in Brescia in 1535, had become in less than a hundred years the Order of Saint Ursula, raised to monastic status with solemn vows and cloister. This monastic pattern, so dissimilar to Angela's original model, was to shape and control a large segment of Ursuline life for the next three hundred fifty years.

One factor remained constant, however: the Company's teaching apostolate. Despite the rigors of cloister, the nuns arranged their monasteries so that boarders could be housed and day students accommodated without violating the rules of cloister. It was undoubtedly this blend of the contemplative and the apostolic that led to their rapid growth not only in France but throughout Europe. By the eighteenth century the Ursuline monasteries in France numbered in the hundreds and most countries on the continent (Holland, Belgium, Poland, Austria, Germany, Hungary, Yugoslavia, Bohemia, Slovakia, Greece) had convents of Ursulines, prized for their schools.

Although the French Revolution (1789) and the turmoil throughout Europe which followed in its wake, devastated religious life, less than fifty years later the French Ursulines had sufficiently reestabilized to engage in a wave of missionary activity. Such missionary activity was not entirely new. As early as 1639 Marie de l'Incarnation, a religious of the monastery of Tours, set out with two companions for the missions of North America. Landing in Quebec in August of that year, they began their work of education with the Indian and the French children of the small wilderness settlement. Thus was established the first convent of nuns and the first Catholic school in North America.

It would be almost a hundred years before another such settlement was made—this time in the southernmost section of what is now the United States: Louisiana. In February 1727, nine Ursulines from various French monasteries set out from Hennebont, a port city in northwest France, and arrived at their destination—New Orleans—five months later. The history of the Ursuline monastery in New Orleans is among the most fascinating and best documented narratives in the history of religious women in America. Despite the difficulties of climate and the turmoil of political upheaval (French territory when the nuns arrived in 1727, the area was ceded to Spain in 1763, then returned to France and finally purchased by the United States in 1803), the nuns were not only able to establish a highly successful school but from this original monastery were founded a number of houses in Texas as well as foundations in Cuba (1804) and in Mexico (1892).

The greatest period of missionary expansion, however, occurred in the mid-nineteenth century, centering largely in Ohio, Missouri, and Kentucky. Within a space of thirteen years (1845–1858), four major Ursuline foundations were established from which dozens of daughter houses would spring. The first of these foundations was made in the rural area of Brown County, Ohio, not far from Cincinnati. Through Bishop Purcell of Cincinnati and Father Rappe, his missionary assistant, eleven Ursulines from Beaulieu and Boulogne-sur-mer (convents only recently reestablished after the horrors of the French Revolution) set sail from Le Havre in May 1845. Five years later Boulogne was again asked for volunteers for the Ohio mission. This time four sisters, accompanied by a laywoman (who in time would become an Ursuline), sailed for America and established a foundation in the little town of Cleveland on the banks of Lake Erie. From these two foundations were to spring houses across Ohio—in Toledo, Youngstown, Cincinnati, and as far west as California, Montana, and Alaska, where they established missions to the native peoples.

At the same time, Ursulines from Germany were also being called to the New World. In 1848, three Ursulines from Straubing in Bavaria arrived in Louisville, Kentucky, at the invitation of Bishop Spalding, who was particularly concerned for the education of his German-speaking parishioners. Further west, in St. Louis, Missouri, Bishop Kenrick also invited German nuns to help with his diocese. In 1848, two Ursulines from Oedenburg (Hungary) and a postulant from Landshut (Bavaria) began their missionary work which, in a few years, would bring them east to the port city of New York and a flowering of Ursulines along the eastern seaboard.

Meanwhile in Canada, the original settlement of Quebec expanded into a vast monastery with daughter houses in several areas of French-speaking Canada. By mid-century English-speaking Canada also welcomed its Ursulines. In 1860, several sisters from the French convent of Le Faouët in Brittany made a foundation in Chatham, Ontario, which would become the mother house for the Chatham Union, comprising convents as far west as Calgary, Alberta. Canada was to be further enriched in the first quarter of the twentieth century by several groups of German Ursulines, who settled in the province of Saskatchewan, and by Ursulines from Belgium, who opened houses in Winnipeg in 1914 and expanded to the East Coast of the United States ten years later.

Thus, in less than fifty years, Ursulines had spread from coast to coast across North America. Although the demands of the pioneer apostolate in the New World bore little resemblance to the well-ordered monastic schools of Europe, the nuns continued to follow, as faithfully as possible, the monastic discipline of the houses from which they had been founded. Despite the haphazard nature of mission living, they adhered to the strict customs brought with them from the motherland: the rules of cloister, the daily recitation of the Office in choir, the long hours of meditative prayer. These women were proud of their Ursuline heritage and jealous to guard it in its entirety. What seems to have been forgotten, however, is the original vision of their foundress—a vision far less cumbersome but equally demanding. The recovery of this vision was to be the work of another century.

Before that was to happen, however, another movement, a movement initiated by the forces of history, was to add a new dimension to Ursuline life. Ursuline monasteries from their origin had been autonomous. Although related through a common foundress and a similar pattern of life, each monastery was an independent, self-sustaining unit. But in the last quarter of the nineteenth century, political events in Europe, with their strong spirit of anticlericalism, made it clear that mutual support across national lines might be the only way to ensure the survival of imperiled monasteries. Thus was born the movement toward unity which in time would extend far beyond Europe and be known as the Roman Union of Ursulines.

This call to unity was variously received. Some houses accepted it eagerly as an enriching contact with other Ursulines; others, often upon the advice of their bishops, felt that they would function best in their local settings without the constraints of a far-off central government. Whatever the response to the Roman Union, it became clear that, with improved communications and more complex apostolic demands, isolation and autonomy would best be replaced by a spirit of closer unity among Ursuline houses.

That such unity, especially in North America, developed so rapidly and with such mutual benefit is due in large part to Vatican II. When John XXIII announced his intention of "opening windows" for the Church, no segment of that Church was more ready to breathe the fresh air that came pouring in than religious women in America. No radical change is ever accomplished with unblemished grace and religious women (even Ursulines!) took their full measure of awkward falls. But despite their stumblings and missteps, one single-minded quest continued unswervingly: the search for their original charism.

Thus Angela Merici has begun to emerge—that single-hearted woman of Brescia whose vision was too pure to admit the clutter of inconsequential or petty directives. To be faithful in one's consecration to Jesus Christ; this was the only essential. All the rest would become luminously clear in the light of this single intention. Thus the accretions of generations have begun to slip away and essential words are being reinterpreted: prayer, cloister, community, are emerging from their narrow bonds, reformulated in the light of the Gospel. Education, so long defined as the specific activities of the classroom, is now seen in its full dimension. "Teaching girls" gives way to the broader concept of "serving women"—and the women who need them are everywhere: in adult education, in childcare centers, in parishes, in campus ministry, in a variety of social services and, of course, in grade schools, high schools, colleges—in classrooms and administration. It is not a question of discarding what has shaped our lives for almost four hundred years; it is simply a matter of reseeing the world and its needs through different eyes—the eyes of Angela to whom we owe our existence.

When the North American Conference of Ursulines Superiors met in London, Ontario, in 1984, they drew up the following statement which expresses the new vision of Angela's daughters:

THE DRIFTWOOD STATEMENT FROM DESENZANO ON LAKE ERIE

We, the members of the North American Conference of Ursuline Superiors, recognize our heritage from the Gospel and from Angela.

To be reconcilors and peacemakers

To be leaven among those with whom we share our global pilgrimage

To be women who are life givers, bringing Christ to an unchristian milieu

By the last decade of the twentieth century, the Ursulines of North America can be found in a wide variety of ministries; but we cannot pride ourselves on breaking new territory, for Angela has done it all before us. We recognize ourselves simply as followers, walking in the footsteps where Angela has led.

Epilogue

Clothed in dignity and power [they] can afford to laugh at tomorrow.

–PROVERBS 31:25

By the last week of July we had finished our task. Our essays had been written and rewritten. Although we knew that we could keep on improving them "for the rest of our lives," as one of our members put it, we knew, too, that it was time to print the final drafts, unplug our computers, and get ready to say our good-byes.

But before that final moment arrived, we knew something else had to happen, something that would symbolize what we had accomplished. How could we ritualize this precious month? Such ritual had to be more than just a bottle of champagne and a festive dinner. It had to be a ritual analogous to our experience. Not an easy call. We needed an IMMENSE experience! And so when someone said, "Let's go to Niagara Falls!" we were ready. Surely that would be big enough and wild enough and free enough!

And so on our last Sunday morning, just as the sun rose, we packed a car and started off on the four-hour drive. We heard the thundering roar of waters long before the hypnotic spectacle of the Falls opened before us. For once the cliché was appropriate: it was, truly, heartstopping.

We did it all that day. We bought tickets for everything. We took our life in our hands and, huddled beneath blue slickers, we boarded the *Maid of the Mist*, that intrepid little boat that dares the currents to the very edge of safety. As we grasped the railing, soaked with spray, watching the roiling waters that surrounded us, we wondered how much further one could go without being lost. Pressed close together, the roar of the waters drowning out our voices, we remembered those inner waters, those bewildering currents which we had faced—and lived.

That afternoon, our energies boundless, we dressed in the requisite yellow slickers and sneakers and climbed down rickety flights of slick wooden stairs until we stood gasping behind the immensity of water that cascaded deafeningly in front of us. But instead of fear, we felt only exultation. The waters had not drowned us. For a month we had let them soak us through, purifying us, enabling us, clarifying our vision. We had let our lives wash over us. We had acknowledged them, claimed them, shared them. And now, at the end, we stood beneath the immensity of water and, like the valiant woman in the Book of Proverbs, we laughed.

About the Contributors

IRENE MAHONEY is a member of the Roman Union Ursulines, Eastern Province, USA. After graduation from the College of New Rochelle, she worked in publishing before entering the Ursuline novitiate in Beacon, New York. She holds a Ph.D. in English and American literature and has taught for a number of years at the college of New Rochelle. In 1980, Irene volunteered for overseas mission service and taught in Taiwan for several years.

Currently she is pursuing her first love: writing. Her published works include three biographies, three novels, and three one-woman plays dealing with the position of women in the Church. Her most recent work is a history of the Ursulines in China.

The Eastern Province Ursulines of the Roman Union were founded in New York City in the mid-nineteenth century by Sisters from Landshut, Bavaria. They presently number about two hundred fifty members and are situated along the Eastern seaboard from the Canadian border to Florida. Their major efforts have been in the field of education, although presently they are also engaged in spiritual direction and retreat work, legal counseling, hospital ministry, and various social action causes. Their members are also at work in Ursuline missions in Africa, India, Thailand, and Guyana.

SHARON SULLIVAN is a Mount Saint Joseph Ursuline of Maple Mount, Kentucky. She is on the faculty of the Division of Education and coordinates the special education program at Brescia College, a Catholic liberal arts college in Owensboro, Kentucky, affiliated with the Mount Saint Joseph Ursulines. Sharon holds a Ph.D. in special education from Purdue University and participates regionally with mild to moderate cognitive disabilities. Sharon is still a Girl Scout and her other principal area of interest involves issues of awareness, education, and service related to the environment.

Within the Ursuline Community, Sharon made her final profession in January 1987. Since then she has served as local coordinator of the Brescia College Community from 1988 to 1990; Chapter delegate or alternate since 1988; member of various ad hoc and chapter committees. Currently she is Chair of the Community Long Range Planning Committee and member of the Stewardship and Resources and Chapter Steering Committees.

The Mount Saint Joseph Ursulines, a community of approximately two hundred forty women religious, were established in 1874 and became an autonomous congregation in 1912. Members currently serve in a variety of ministries, including Catholic education, pastoral ministry, social concerns—women's issues, environmental awareness—and healthcare. They are located throughout the United States, including Kentucky, New Mexico, Missouri, Nebraska, Tennessee, New York, Washington, D.C., and other scattered missions. At present they maintain one mission in Chile.

ROSE-ANNE ENGEL is an Ursuline Sister of Prelate, Saskatchewan in western Canada. She lives in the city of Calgary, Alberta, Canada. Rose-Anne holds degrees in education, religious studies, and law. She is the coordinator of adult-religious education in the Diocese of Calgary and freelances research in law on human rights, ethics, and justice issues. She serves on the Board of Governors of Saint Mary's College and plays the flute in the Calgary Westwinds Concert Band.

Rose-Anne grew up on a farm in Saskatchewan, was a teacher for seventeen years, the religion consultant of the Catholic schools of Saskatoon, Saskatchewan, for eight years, and served on numerous boards for organizations dedicated to justice. She was the general superior of the Ursuline Sisters of Prelate from 1983 to 1991. She has been active in other leadership roles in her Ursuline community, especially at the General Conventions. Rose-Anne loves Ursuline celebrations, reading, music, sports, and family gatherings.

The Ursuline Sisters of Prelate, Saskatchewan in Canada, founded in 1919, are an autonomous community of eighty-three women religious, and are dedicated to "Education for Life." The Ursulines of Prelate serve in diverse ministries including teaching from grade schools through university levels, hold positions of leadership at the diocesan and pastoral level in the Prairie Provinces of Canada, and have served in the missions in Africa and South America. They have a particular emphasis in their ministry on the issues of equality and justice, particularly as they affect women. They have always promoted the arts, especially music and drama. The Ursuline Sisters of Prelate still operate Saint Angela's Academy, a modern, private, residential secondary school in Prelate, Saskatchewan.

DIANNE BAUMUNK is a Roman Union Ursuline of the Western Province, USA. Profession in 1967, Dianne has ministered as high school teacher and principal, retreat house director, pastoral minister, community administrator, and group process facilitator. Many of her years of service have been with Native Americans, both Eskimos and Indians, in Bush Alaska and the Crow Tribe in Montana.

Having a master's degree in applied behavior science from the Leadership Institute of Seattle, Dianne's expertise is in organizational development. Presently, she is principal of Ursuline High School in Santa Rosa, California.

The Western Province Ursulines of the Roman Union consist of fifty-three Sisters ministering in California, Idaho, Montana, and Alaska. While the northern communities of the Province were founded by the Ursulines of Toledo, Ohio, the California foundation began in 1880 by the Ursulines of Brown County, Ohio. With wide geographic spread and diversity of ministry, the Western Province is marked by a continuing pioneer spirit.

SUSAN BREMER has been a member of the Cleveland Ursulines since 1981. The Cleveland native earned undergraduate degrees in English and theology from Ursuline College, Cleveland, and a master of arts degree in pastoral ministry from the University of Dayton, Dayton, Ohio. She has served as a pastoral minister, pastoral care/health aide, and campus minister. Currently, Susan is engaged in public relations and development for the Ursuline Sisters and for two community-affiliated high schools. She is a founding member of WomenWatch, a local organization committed to speaking out against violence, particularly violence against women and children.

The Cleveland Ursulines were established in 1850. Within weeks of their arrival from France, four Sisters opened Ursuline Academy, the first school in the Cleveland diocese. Today, the nearly three-hundred-member community continues to serve the diocese, and since 1968 has had Sisters serve as missionaries in El Salvador. In addition, some Sisters now serve in Mexico, Florida, Montana, Michigan, Massachusetts, Pennsylvania, and Missouri. While education—elementary school through college—continues to be the congregation's primary ministry, Sisters also serve in healthcare, parish and hospital ministry, missionary work, and in organizations dedicated to serving minorities, the economically poor, and those promoting peace and justice.

ADRIANA MENDEZ-PENATE is a Roman Union Ursuline of the Mexican Province. Born in Cuba in 1943, she became a refugee in 1961, following the Castro takeover. For two years she lived and worked in New York City before entering the Ursuline novitiate in Puebla in 1963. Within the Ursuline community Adriana has served as teacher, rural parish worker, novice directress, and provincial.

Currently, Adriana lives and works in a parish in Cuernavaca in the state of Morelos. Together with her small community she is involved in evangelization, catechetical work, writing, and Bible courses from women's perspective. She is also studying open theology at the Jesuit University.

The Province of Mexico was founded in Puebla in 1892 by three sisters from San Antonio and Laredo, Texas. In 1900 the community joined the recently established Roman Union of Ursulines. Today the province consists of four houses in the states of Puebla, Guerrero, Morelos, and Tabasco. There are presently thirty-five sisters in the province with seven junior professed, two novices, and two postulants. All are engaged in education and evangelization in schools and parishes.

MARY CABRINI DURKIN is an Ursuline of Cincinnati. She has been a teacher of English, Latin, journalism, and humanities at Saint Ursula Academy there. In 1991, she was elected superior of her congregation, after several terms as councilor.

Among other civic involvements, Mary Cabrini has headed the Cincinnati chapter of Bread for the World. Her inter-Ursuline activities include co-chairing the 1991 North American Conference of Ursuline Education, serving on the board of Ursuline Companions in Mission, and publishing a semi-annual newsletter, *Quilt-Threads*.

The Ursulines of Cincinnati, Ohio, a small autonomous congregation, were founded in 1910. As educators, they established and served in many parish schools in southwest Ohio and in two private schools, which they continue to sponsor. Today the Sisters strive to carry a gospel presence into a variety of works and neighborhoods. They have recently begun to explore ways of nurturing new forms of Ursuline life rooted in Saint Angela's vision of the original (1535) Company of Saint Ursula.

HEDWIG OWSIAK is a member of the Tildonk Congregation of Ursulines. Born in Norwich, Connecticut, she attended school and college in West Hartford. In 1956, she entered the Ursuline novitiate and made her first vows in 1959. After completing a master's degree in philosophy at Saint John's University in Jamaica, Long Island, she traveled to Belgium where she studied theology at Lumen Vitae.

Upon returning to America, Heddie served as diocesan co-ordinator at parent and sacrament programs. In 1975, she became provincial superior of the U.S. Province. She held this post for three years and in 1978 became assistant to the superior general, a position she has filled until the summer of 1996.

The Ursulines of Tildonk were founded by Father John Lambertz in Tildonk, Belgium, in 1818. Although houses were originally independent, convents began to group themselves around the mother house of Tildonk by 1895, when the first superior general was elected. Today they number almost eight hundred Sisters and are located in Belgium, the United States, Canada, India, and Zaire.